THE
EVERYTHING
KAKURO
CHALLENGE
BOOK

Dear Reader,

Welcome to kakuro, the latest puzzle craze to sweep the world! This book provides a range of challenges, from mild to extreme. Like all good puzzles, kakuro takes only a minute to learn. Like only the very best puzzles, you can spend a lifetime solving kakuro and still find it intriguing. But be warned: Kakuro is one of the most addicting puzzles out there!

Until recently, kakuro has been a well-kept secret among serious puzzle players. This is a shame because kakuro can be fun for everyone, and genius-level IQs are definitely not required! You don't even need to be a whiz with numbers to solve kakuro. And being good at crossword puzzles probably won't help you much either, even though the puzzles look similar. More than anything, kakuro requires logical reasoning. And sharpening our logical reasoning skills is a worthwhile pursuit, especially if we can have a lot of fun at the same time!

Charles Timmerman

THE
EVERYTHING®
KAKURO
CHALLENGE
BOOK

Over **200** tough puzzles
with instructions for solving

Charles Timmerman
Author of *The Everything® Giant Sudoku Book*
and founder of Funster.com

Adams Media
New York   London   Toronto   Sydney   New Delhi

*Dedicated to the memory of Grandma Timmerman
who was once the best in her class with numbers.*
• • •

Publishing Director: Gary M. Krebs
Associate Managing Editor: Laura M. Daly
Associate Copy Chief: Brett Palana-Shanahan
Acquisitions Editor: Kate Burgo
Development Editor: Jessica LaPointe
Associate Production Editor: Casey Ebert

Director of Manufacturing: Susan Beale
Associate Director of Production: Michelle Roy Kelly
Cover Design: Paul Beatrice, Erick DaCosta,
  Matt LeBlanc
Layout and Graphics: Colleen Cunningham,
  Holly Curtis, Sorae Lee

An Everything® Series Book.
Everything® and everything.com® are registered trademarks of Simon & Schuster, Inc.

Published by Adams Media, an Imprint of Simon & Schuster, Inc.
100 Technology Center Drive, Stoughton, MA 02072 U.S.A.
www.adamsmedia.com

ISBN 13: 978-1-59869-057-6
ISBN 10: 1-59869-057-4

Printed in the United States of America.

J I H G F E D C

This publication is designed to provide accurate and authoritative information with regard to the subject matter covered. It is sold with the understanding that the publisher is not engaged in rendering legal, accounting, or other professional advice. If legal advice or other expert assistance is required, the services of a competent professional person should be sought.
—From a *Declaration of Principles* jointly adopted by a Committee of the American Bar Association and a Committee of Publishers and Associations

Many of the designations used by manufacturers and sellers to distinguish their products are claimed as trademarks. Where those designations appear in this book and Adams Media was aware of a trademark claim, the designations have been printed with initial capital letters.

*This book is available at quantity discounts for bulk purchases.
For information, please call 1-800-289-0963.*

CONTENTS

ACKNOWLEDGMENTS

A special thanks to Thomas and Nancy Westbom whose expertise and assistance made this book possible. And thanks to each of the half a million or so people who have visited my Web site, *www.funster.com*, to play word games and puzzles. You are the inspiration for this book. Much appreciation goes to my agent Jacky Sach, whose e-mail from out of the blue started me down this amusing path of writing puzzle books. I am truly grateful to the people at Adams Media for providing this opportunity. In particular, the puzzles look even better thanks to technical help from Matt LeBlanc. And it was a pleasure working with my editors, Kate Burgo, Jessica LaPointe, and Kate Powers, who provided expert guidance and support. But most of all, thanks to Suzanne and Calla for all the good times!

Introduction
The History of Kakuro

Kakuro was born in America and later acquired a Japanese name. It first appeared in 1966 in an American puzzle magazine published by Dell Magazines. They gave it the name "Cross Sums," which is still used today. In fact, these puzzles have always been popular with hardcore puzzlers. Recently cross sums (or kakuro) puzzles have gained more of a mainstream following.

In 1980 a Japanese man named Maki Kaji was in the United States on business. A puzzle connoisseur, he naturally sampled some of the local fare. The ubiquitous crossword puzzles were not to his liking as his English was not all that good. However, he was able to devour cross sum puzzles right away as they contained only numbers. Maki was so taken with the puzzle that he started creating and publishing them back in Japan. He renamed the puzzle *kasan kurosu*, a combination of the Japanese word for "addition" and the Japanese pronunciation of the English word "cross." Soon it was abbreviated to *kakuro*, or sometimes *kakro*. Within a few years it became a craze in puzzle-obsessed Japan. Maki and his company Nikoli went on to sell about one million kakuro books.

Interestingly, kakuro has followed a course similar to its popular cousin, sudoku. Sudoku is also a puzzle that was invented in the United States and then made popular under a different name in Japan. The next step in both puzzles' conquest was England, another country filled with puzzle lovers. First sudoku and then kakuro were printed in British newspapers and popular books. As for the rest of the world, sudoku has led the way to an increased interest in puzzles across the globe. Following right along, kakuro is gaining fans all over the world including back in the United States where it began.

The Rules of Kakuro

Kakuro is played on a grid that looks much like a crossword puzzle. In kakuro, the clues are sums located above or to the left of each entry. The object is to fill in the blank squares using the numbers 1 to 9 so that they add up to the sums. No number can be used more than once in a sum. There will always be just one solution for each puzzle.

How to Solve Kakuro Puzzles

There are many ways to solve a kakuro puzzle. This section explains the basic strategy to get you started. No doubt you will discover more techniques as you become a kakuro master.

Sum Combinations

Here's a quick puzzle: What three numbers from 1 to 9 will add up to 7 without repeating any number? In this case, there is only one answer: 1+2+4=7. So if a kakuro puzzle has 3 spaces and requires a sum of 7, then the numbers must be a 1, a 2, and a 4. We do not know the order of these numbers, but we will deal with this detail later. The table in Appendix B lists all of the possible combinations for any given number of spaces and sums. This table tells us the possible numbers for any entry in a kakuro puzzle.

In many cases there are numerous possible combinations of numbers and the numbers can be arranged in any order. So this table will not really tell us all of the answers, of course. But it does give us a good starting point to work from. The real trick is to use logic to determine what number must go where. This is usually done by the process of elimination. Answers are determined by ruling out all but one possibility.

Learning By Example

This example will illustrate the basic approach to solving kakuro puzzles. We will completely solve a smaller kakuro puzzle. The same strategies can be used in various ways to solve the puzzles in this book.

First we will determine AB in Figure 1-1. Using the table in Appendix B (or our own reasoning) we know that the three number entry for the sum of 7 down must be 1, 2, and 4 (1+2+4). Similarly, the two number entry for the sum of 4 across must be 1 and 3 (1+3). These two entries intersect at B and have only one number in common: a 1. Therefore, B must be a 1. No other number will work for both the down and across sums. It is easy to see that A must now be a 3, so that A+B will equal 4.

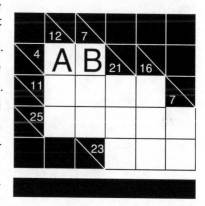

Moving on, let's determine CD in Figure 1-2. We know that C must be either a 2 or a 4 to complete the sum of 7 down. Let's try to find a clue to help us pick one of these two numbers for C. Notice the four number entry for the sum of 11 across must be 1, 2, 3, 5. Since C is one of these digits, we must pick the 2 because the 4 is not possible. And D must be a 4, to complete the sum for 7 down.

It is now possible to figure out EFG in Figure 1-3. From our previous entry, we know that E must be a 1, 5, or 3 as part of the sum of 11 across. There are multiple possibilities for the three number entry for the sum of 21 down: 4, 8, 9; 5, 7, 9; or 6, 7, 8. We can see that E must be

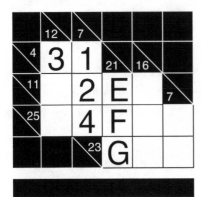

a 5, because it is the only number in common with both the across sum and the possible down sums. This means that the entry for the sum of 21 down can only be 5, 7, 9. Let's determine if G is the remaining 7 or 9. The three number entry for the sum of 23 across must be 6, 8, 9. So G must be a 9, because it is the only number that will work for both the across sum and the down sum. Obviously F must be a 7 to complete the sum for 21 down.

Now we can determine HJK in Figure 1-4. Since H is part of the sum of 11 across, it must be either the remaining 1 or 3. We can rule out the 3 because it is already found in the box above H. Of course, numbers can only be used once in any sum. Thus, H must be a 1. Therefore, J must be a 3 and K an 8 to complete the sums.

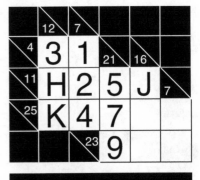

We can figure out entry LMNP in Figure 1-5. There are fully twelve possibilities for a five number entry for the sum of 25 across, but only one of the twelve includes 8, 4, 7, as is required from our previous results. That only possibility is 1, 4, 5, 7, and 8, which leaves either a 1 or a 5 for L. Now let's look at the possibilities for L's column, a three number entry for the sum of 16 down that must include a 3: 3, 4, 9; 3, 5, 8; and 3, 6, 7. This narrows the

possibility for L to just a 5. It is a simple matter to complete the sums: M must be a 1, N an 8, and P a 6.

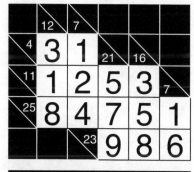

Figure 1-6 shows the completed puzzle. Admittedly, we made this example look somewhat easy by analyzing paths we knew would pay off. In the real world, a lot of trial and error is required to unlock the answers. Your persistence and ingenuity will solve any of these puzzles!

Tips

- Start with the shortest entries.
- Look for the smallest and largest sums, they will have the fewest possible combinations of answers.
- Use the sum combinations table in Appendix B as a starting point to determine the possible combinations for an entry.
- For each space, use the sums from both the row and the column to narrow down the possibilities.
- Write down possible combinations in the margins or on scrap paper.
- Use a pencil and an eraser. Changes are common!
- Don't dwell on just one section of the puzzle, especially if you get stumped.
- Follow the numbers: One answer will often unlock more answers.
- Never give up! Put the board aside and you might be surprised how easy it is to solve later with a fresh look.
- Teach yourself! One of the joys of kakuro is discovering new strategies and methods that work for you.

PUZZLES

Part 1
Mildly Challenging Puzzles

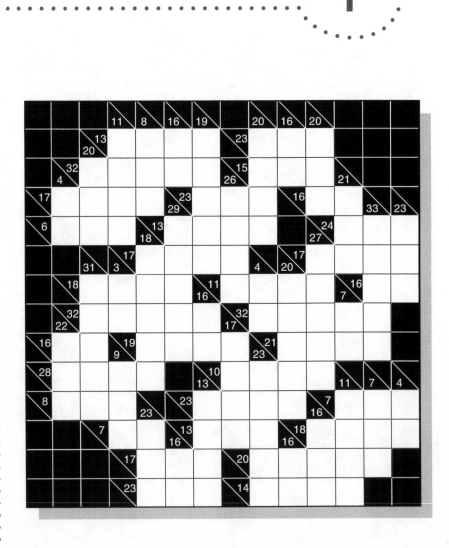

2

3

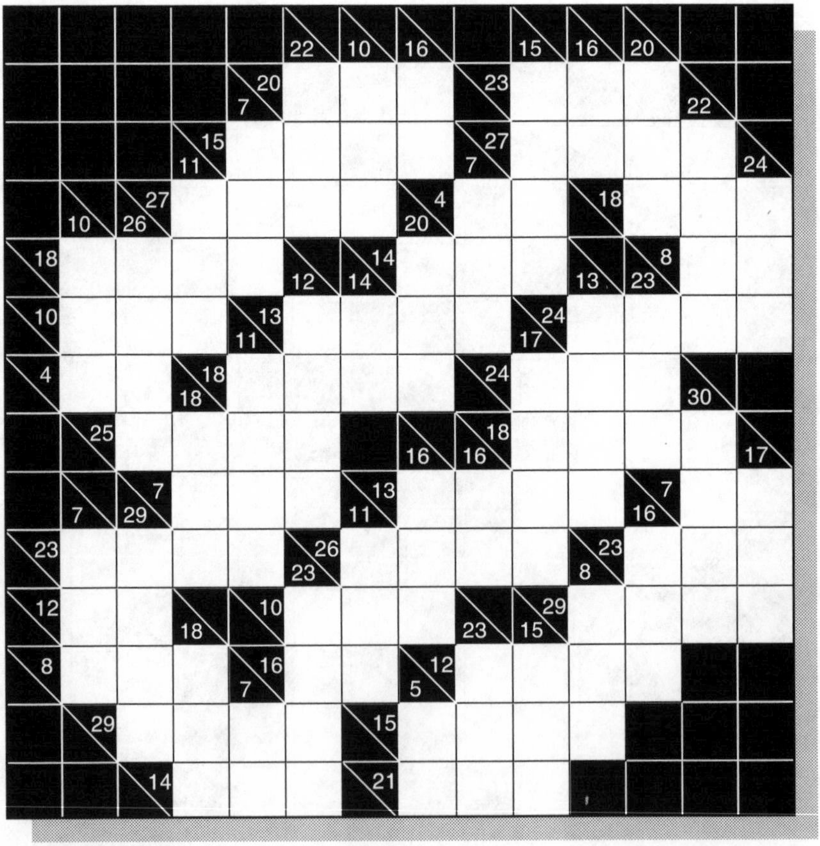

4

5

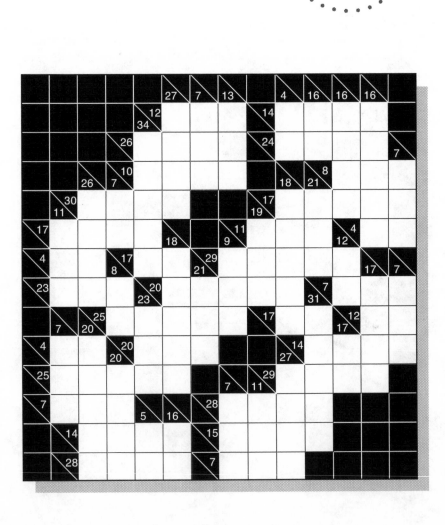

8

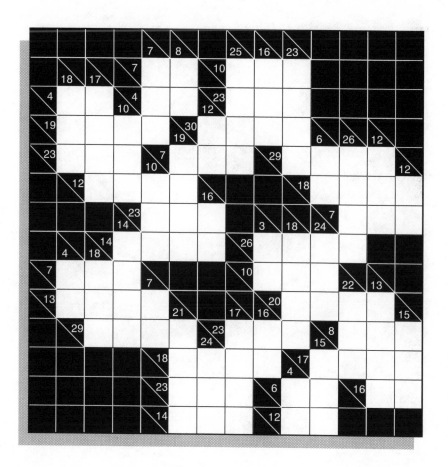

9

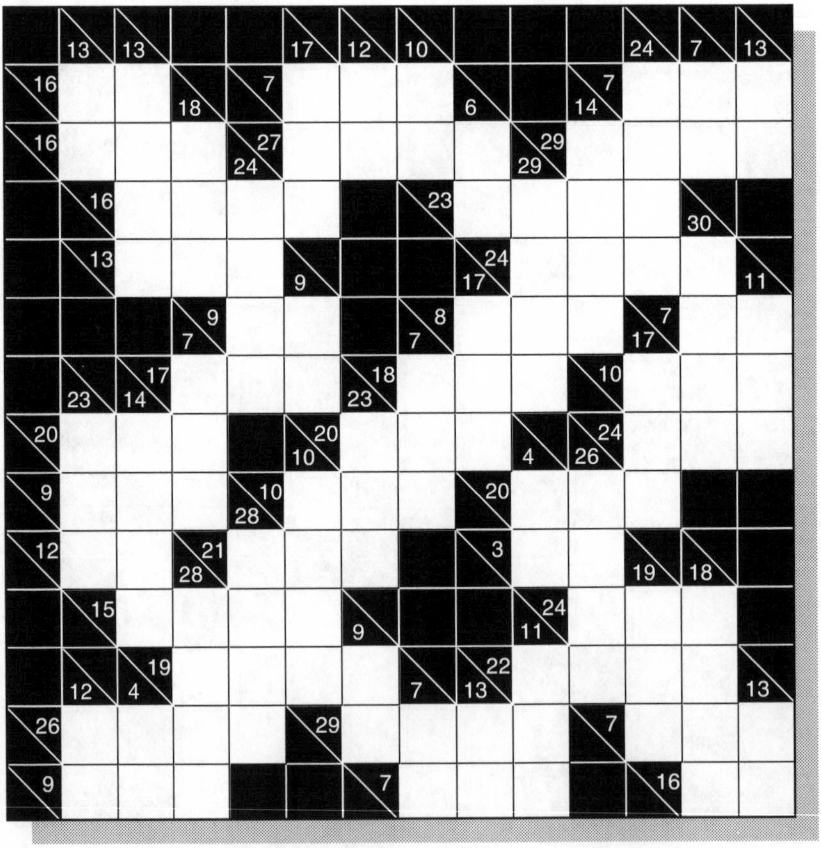

10

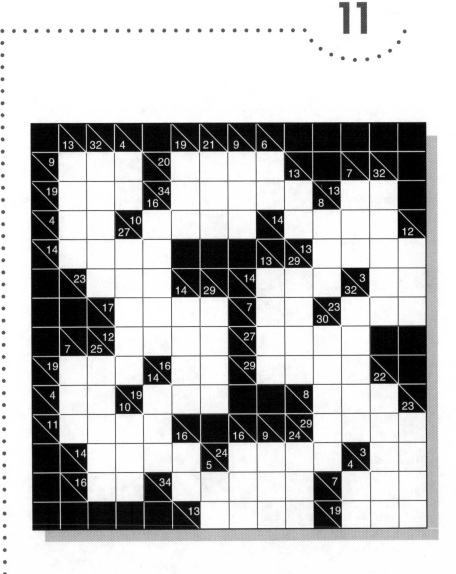

12

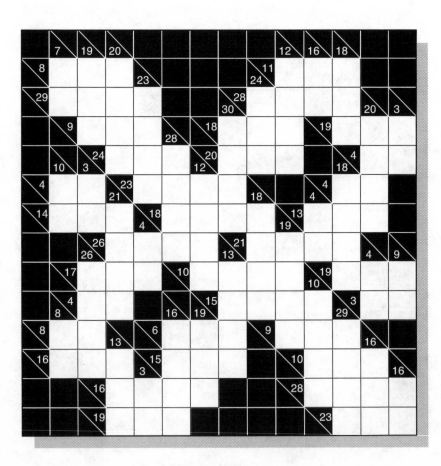

14

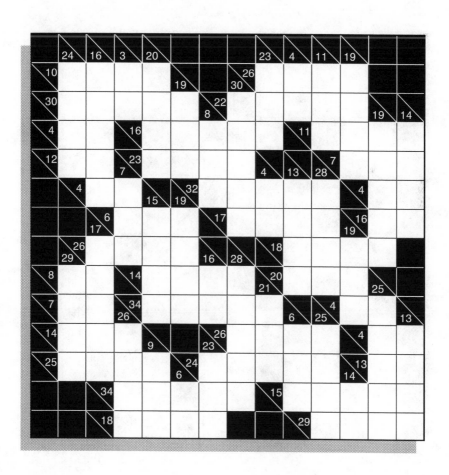

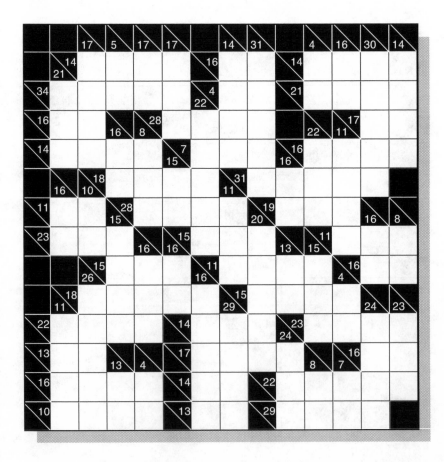

16

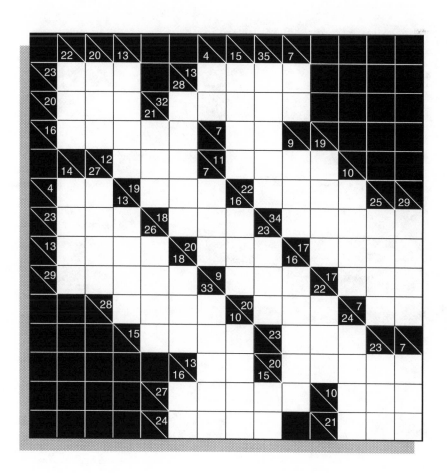

17

20 6 23 7 4 9
22 25 7 27
15 11 16 18 10 6 12
19 13 15 21
16 15 22 6 25 10
11 29 11 7
14 7 29 6
13 3 20 21
7 13 20 4 18 11 30 16
7 11 25 26
20 8 12 8 7 7
12 29 16 18 4
17 23
11 9

18

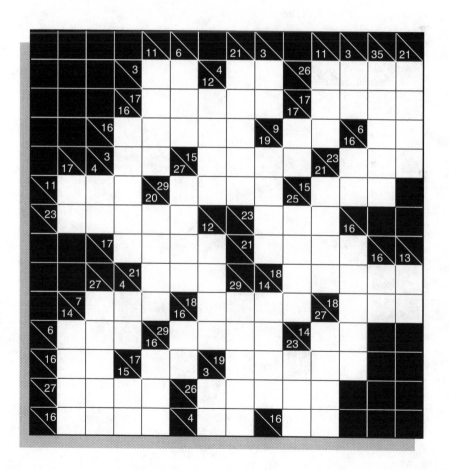

19

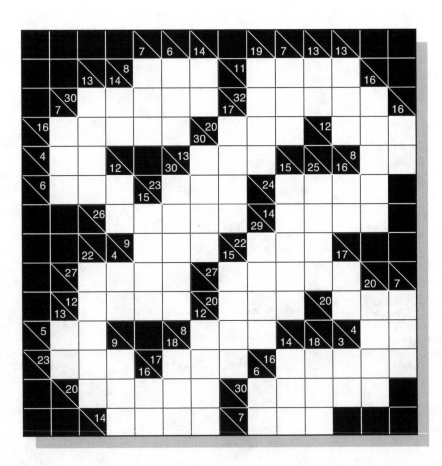

20

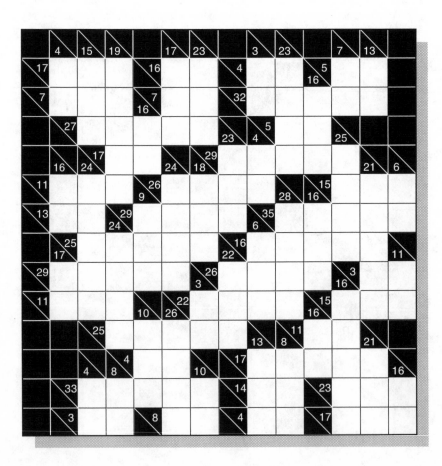

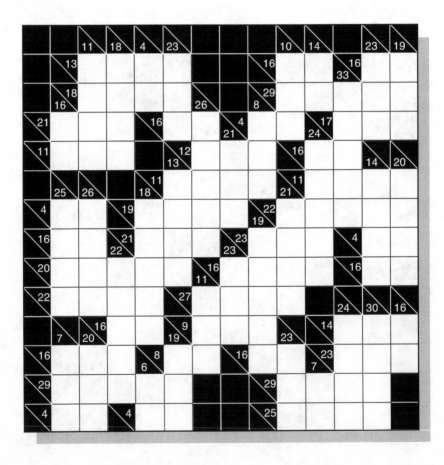

24

26

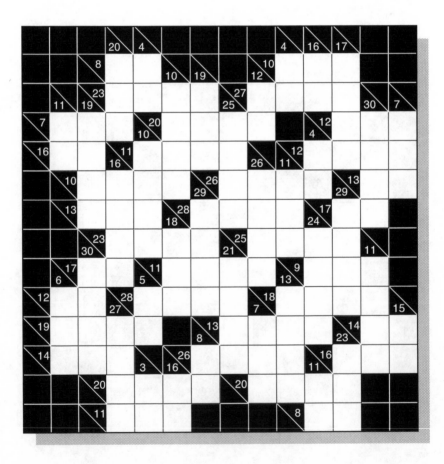

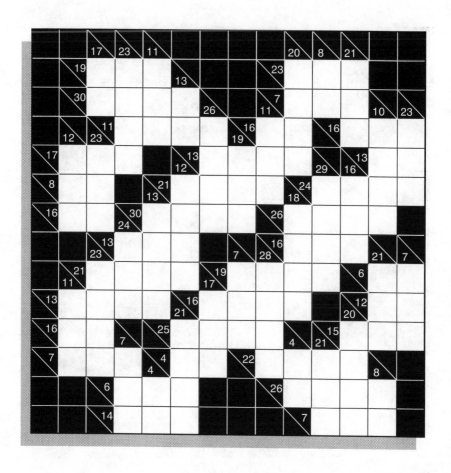

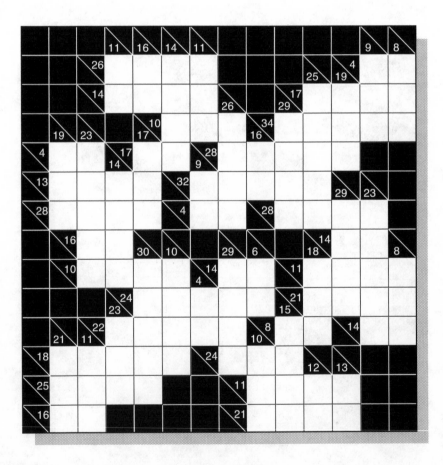

30

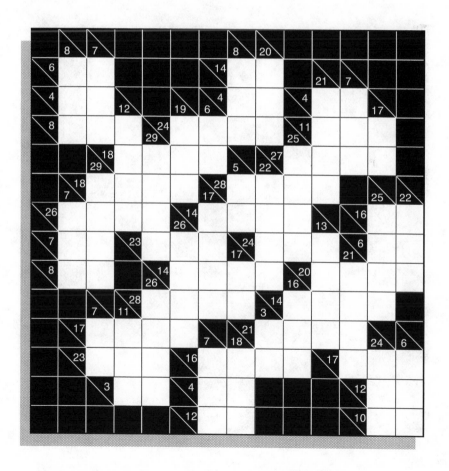

32

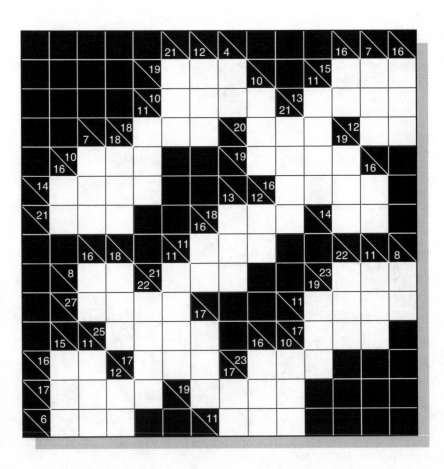

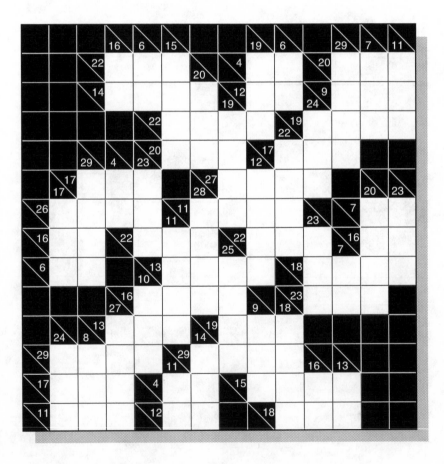

36

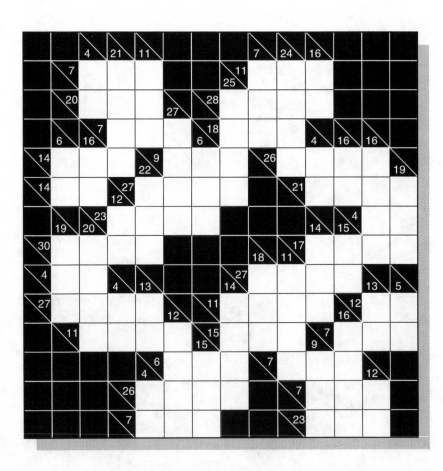

38

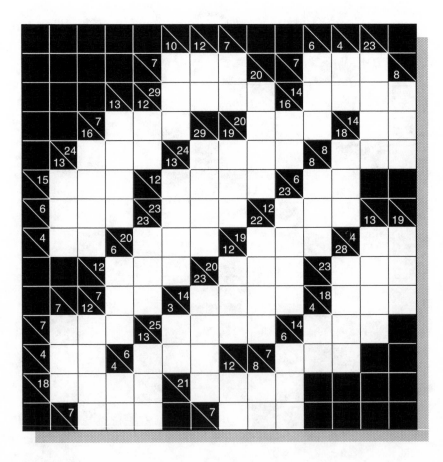

40

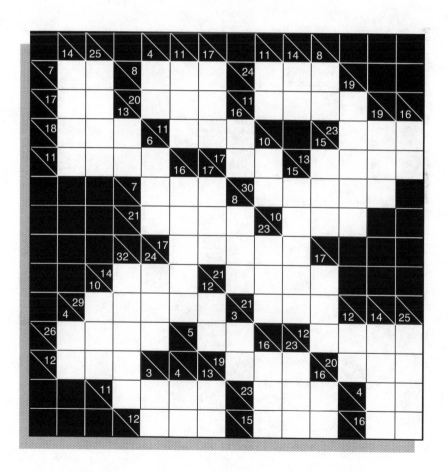

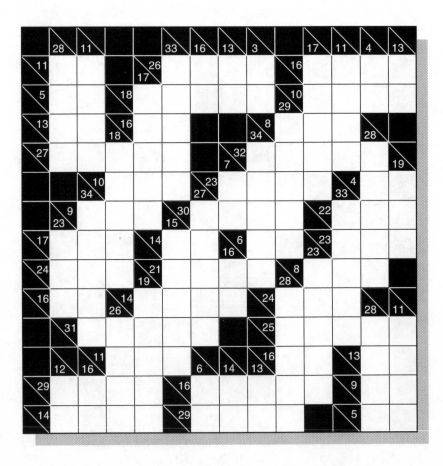

42

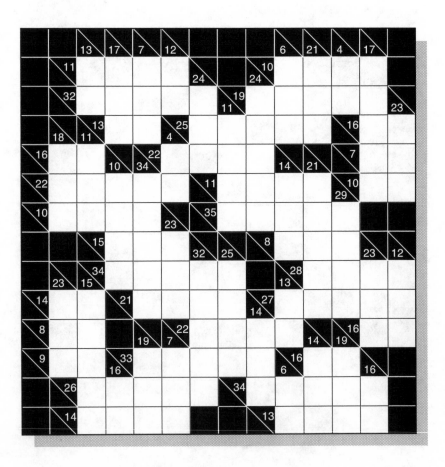

44

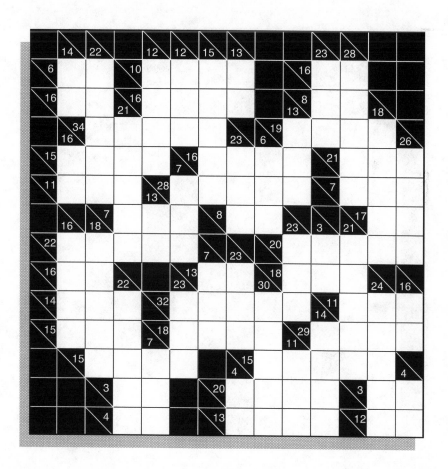

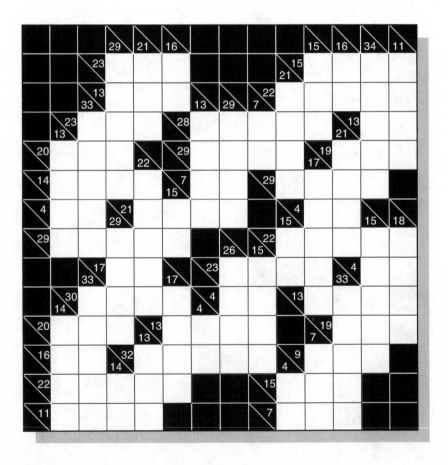

46

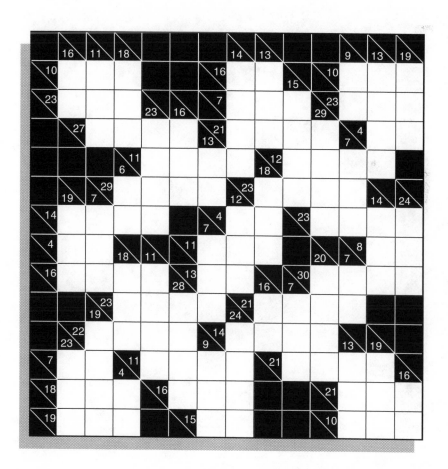

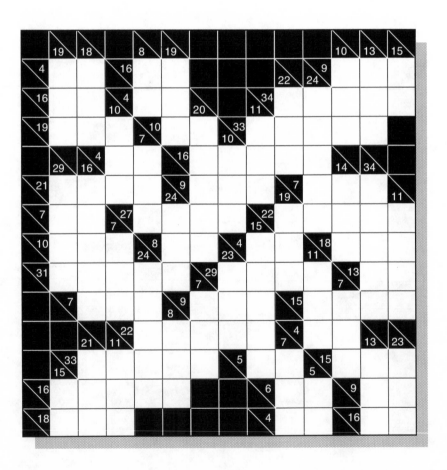

50

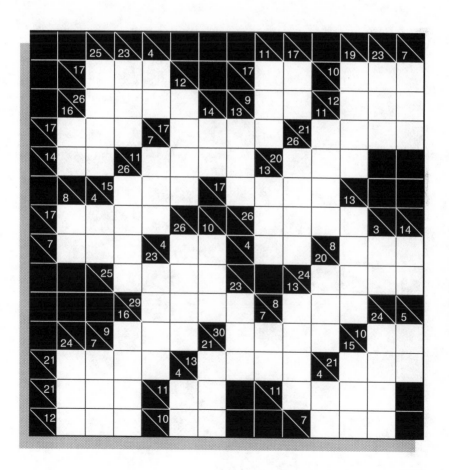

51

52

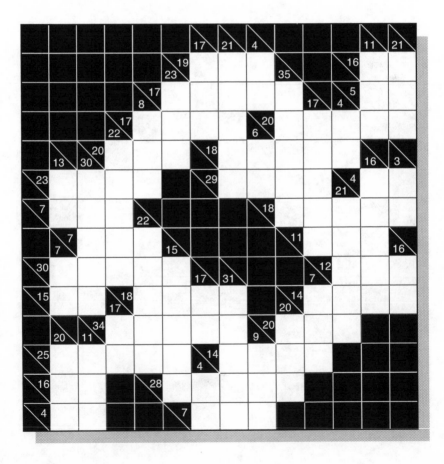

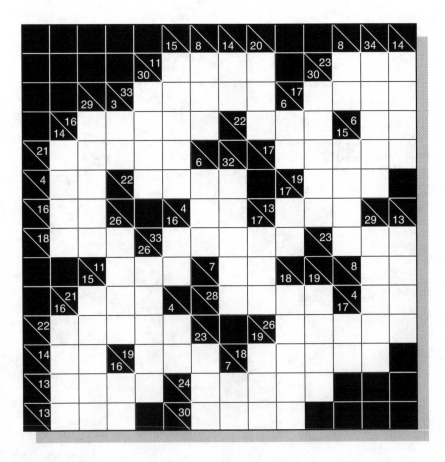

56

58

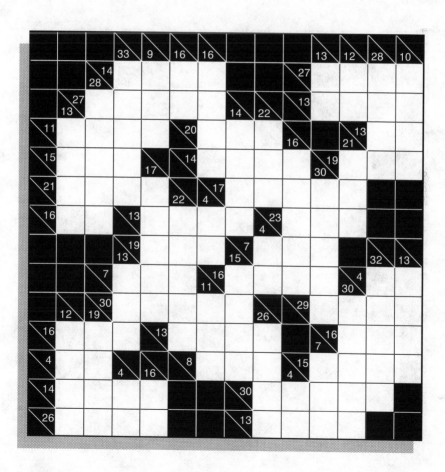

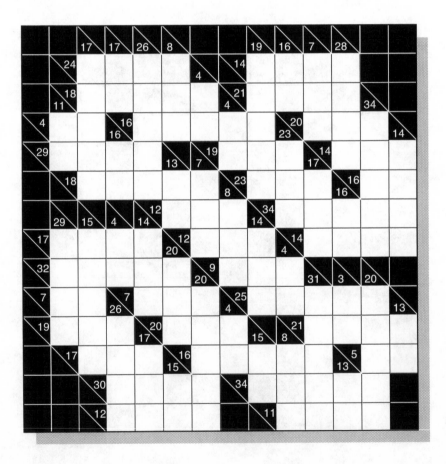

64

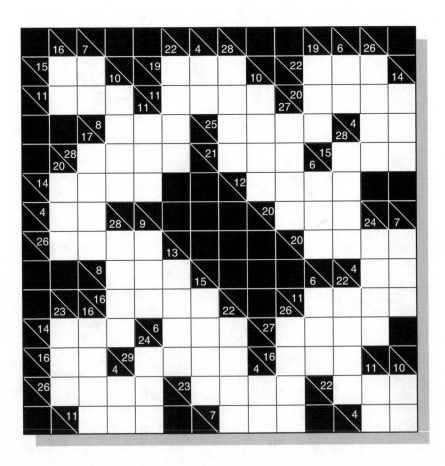

66

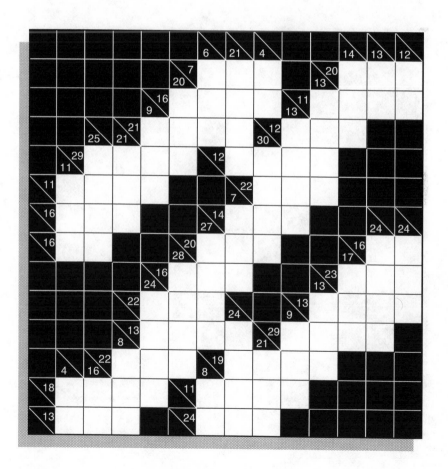

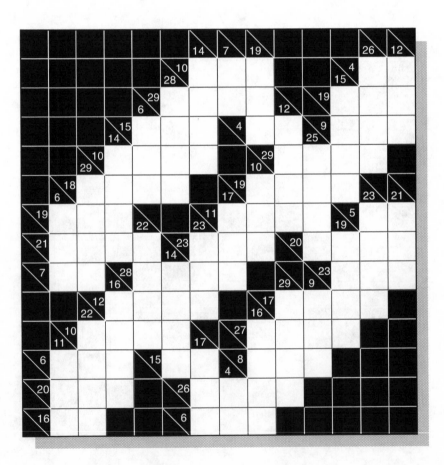

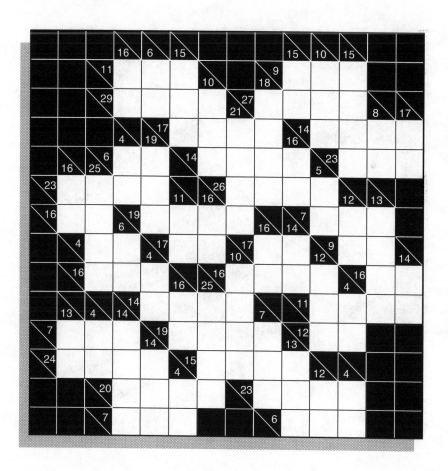

70

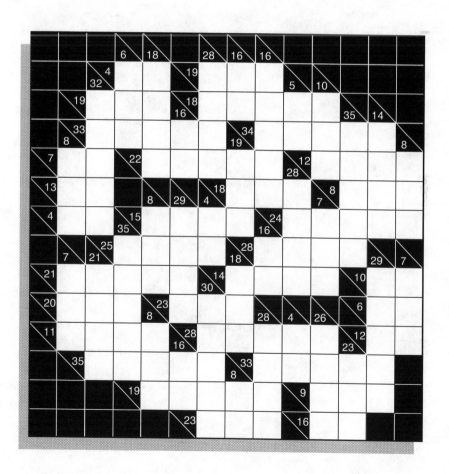

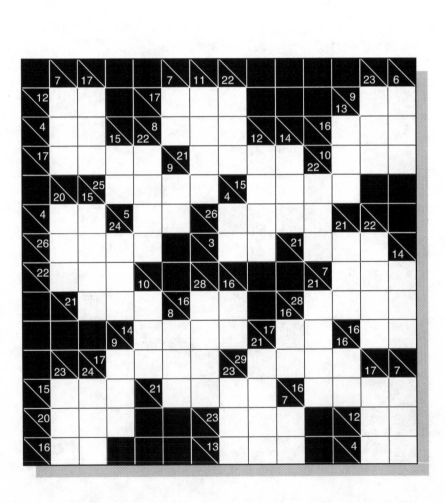

71

72

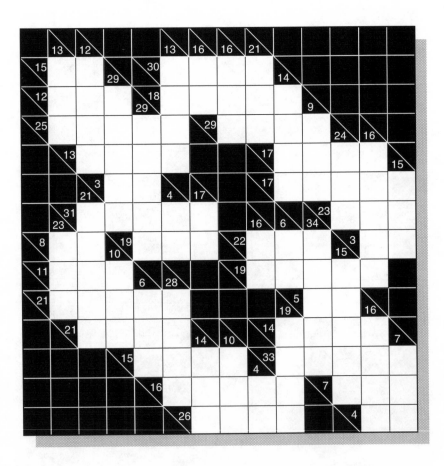

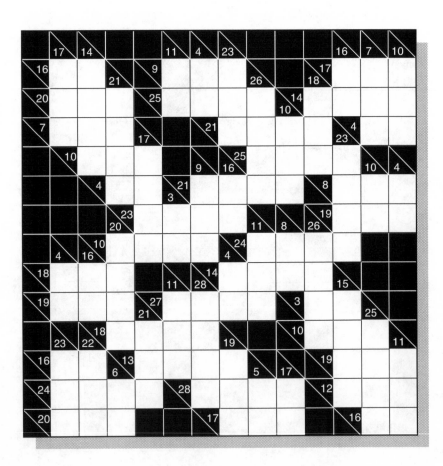

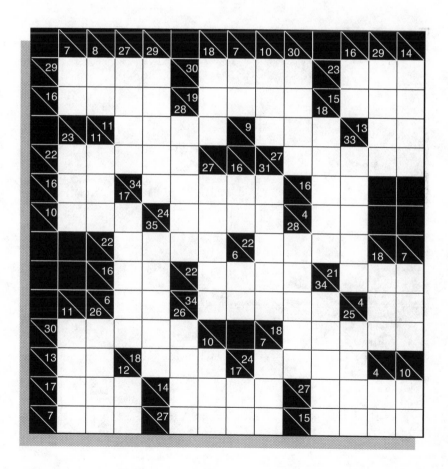

80

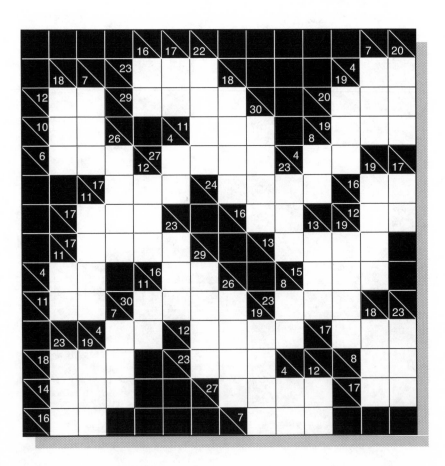

Part 2
Moderately Challenging Puzzles

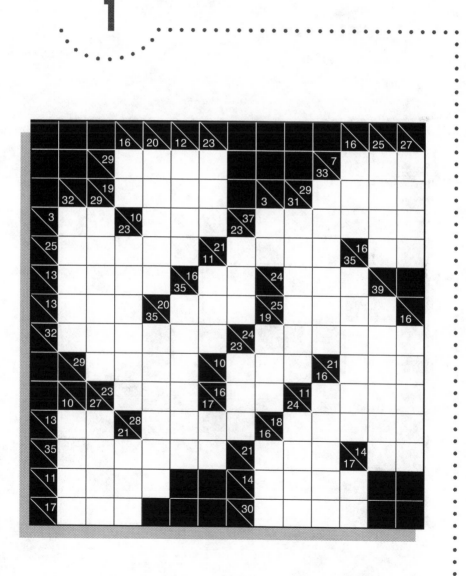

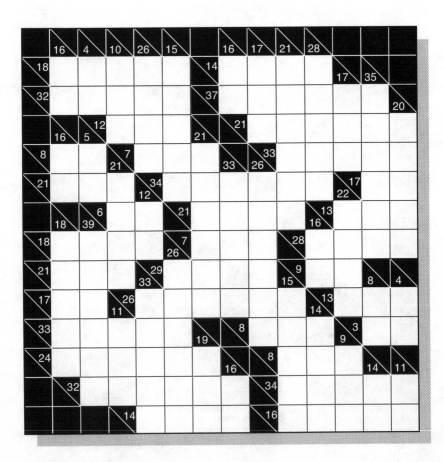

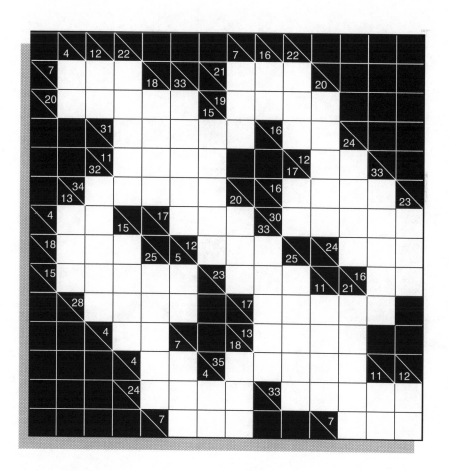

4

5

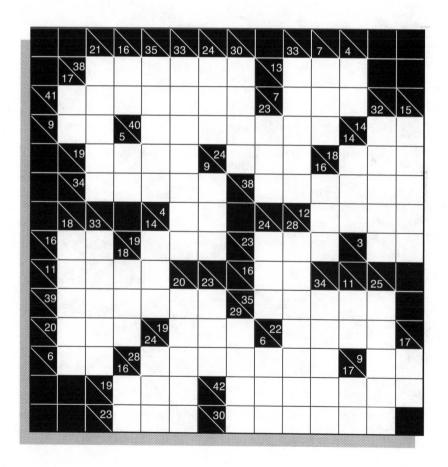

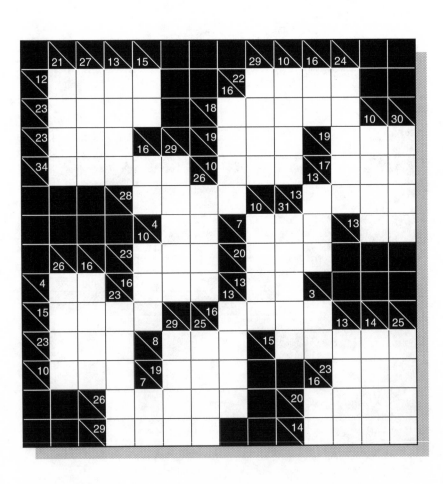

7

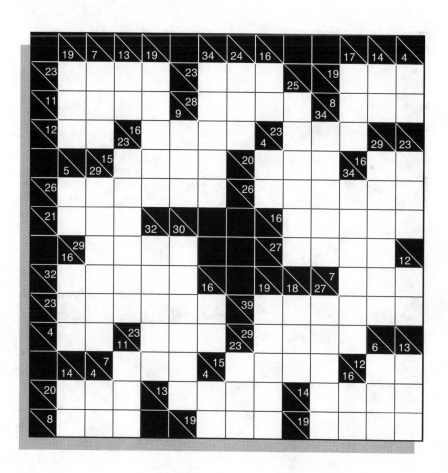

8

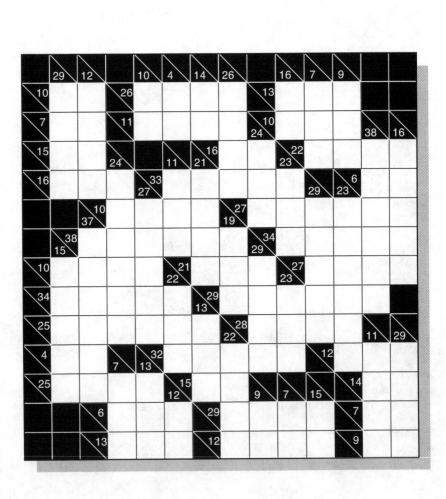

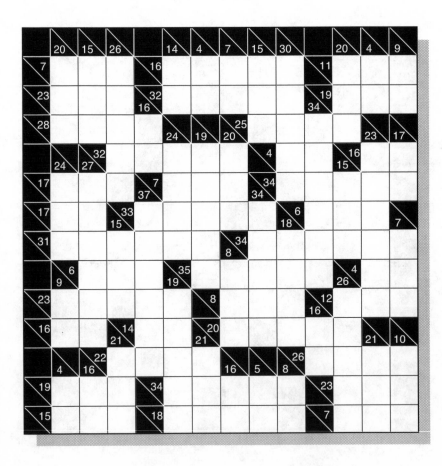

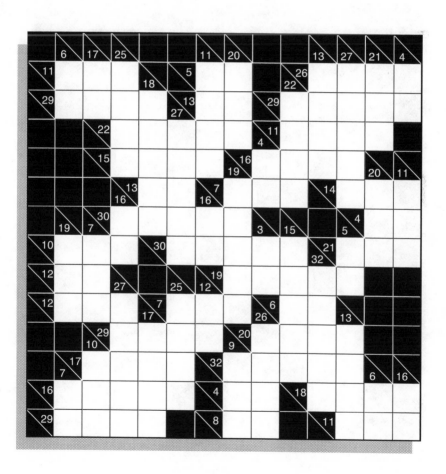

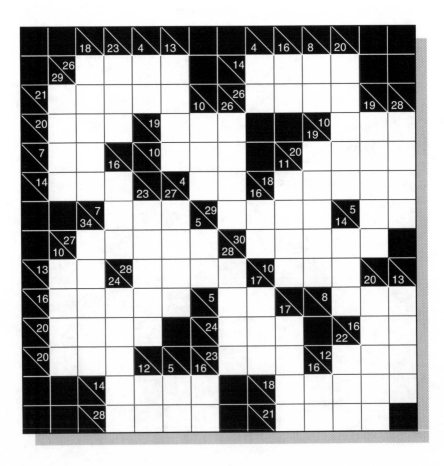

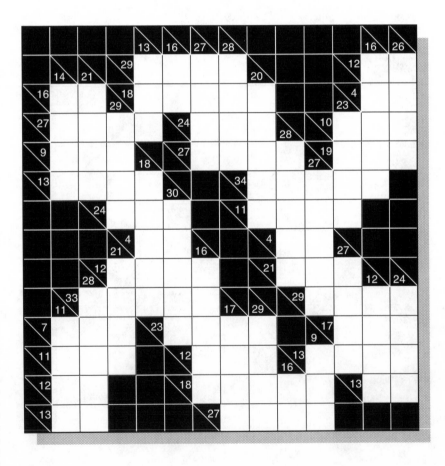

15

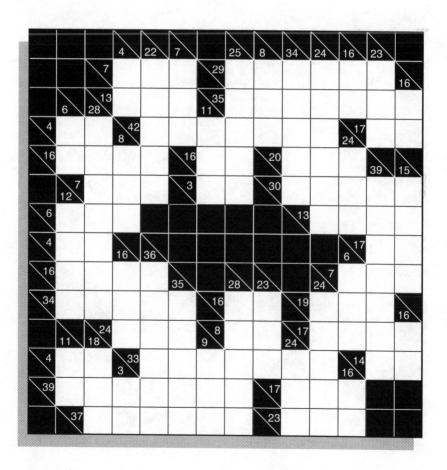

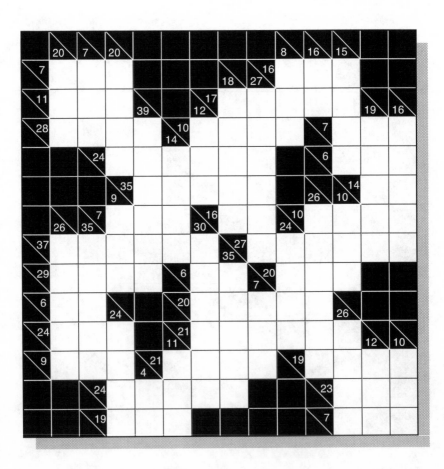

17

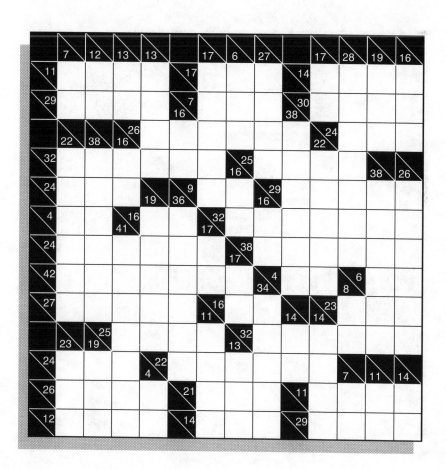

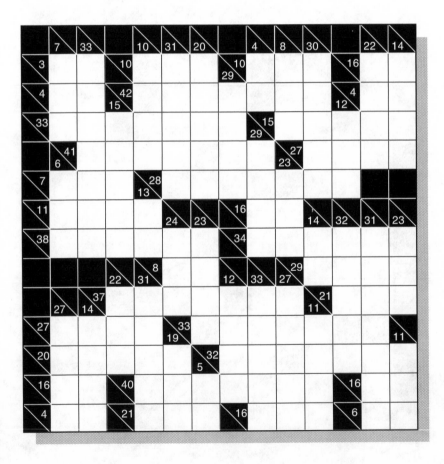

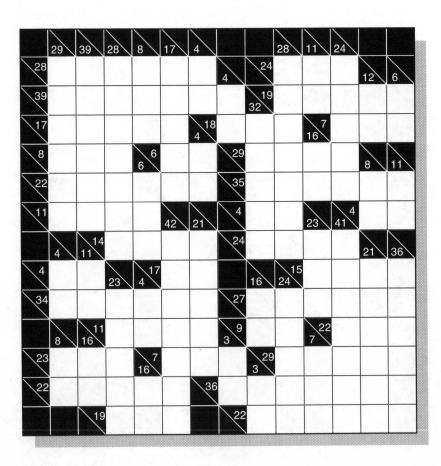

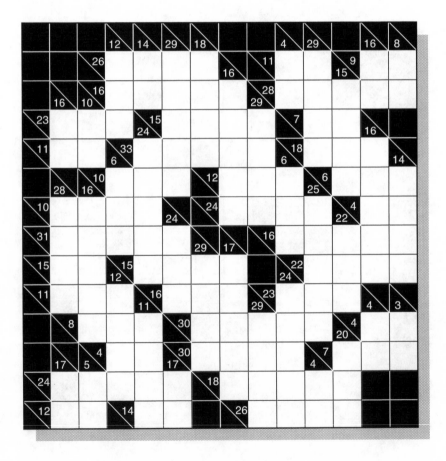

23

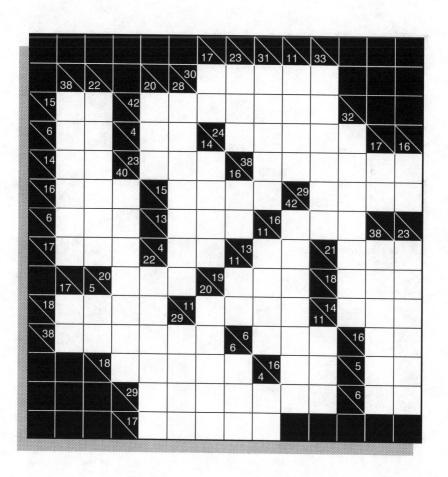

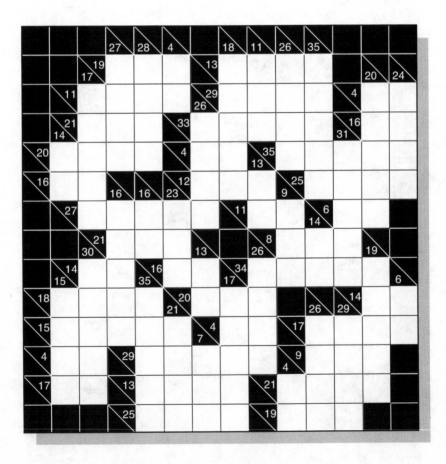

25

26

27

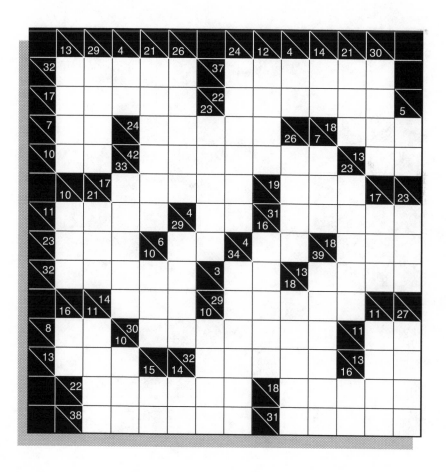

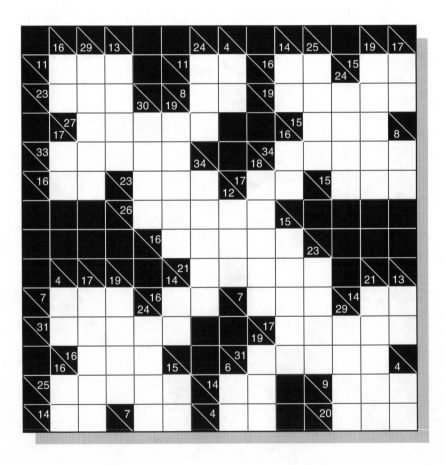

29

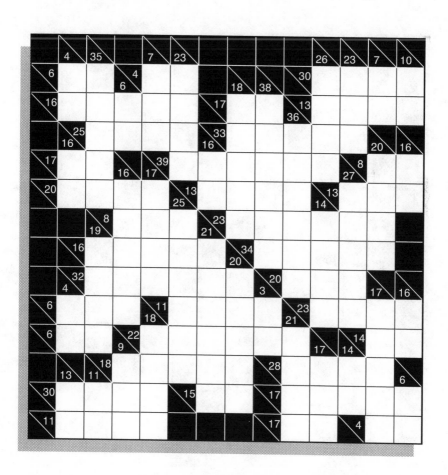

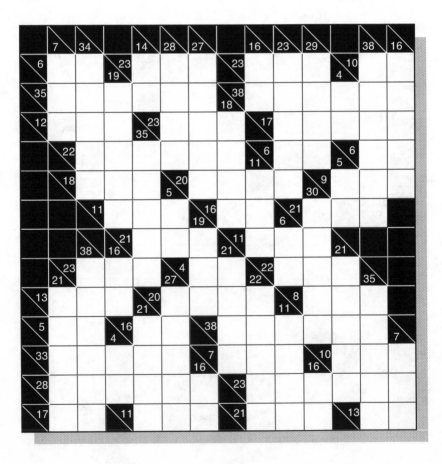

31

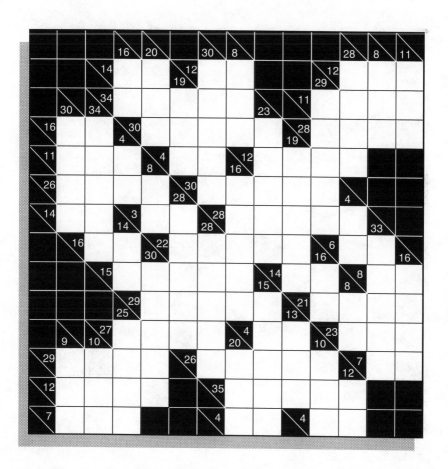

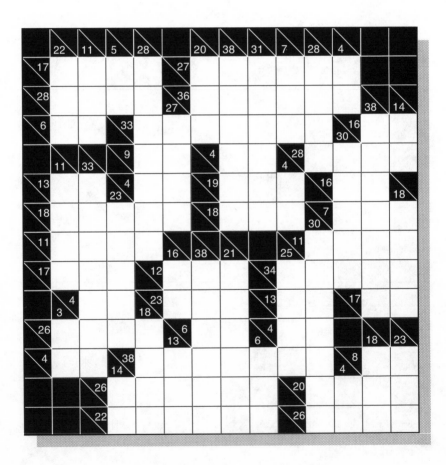

33

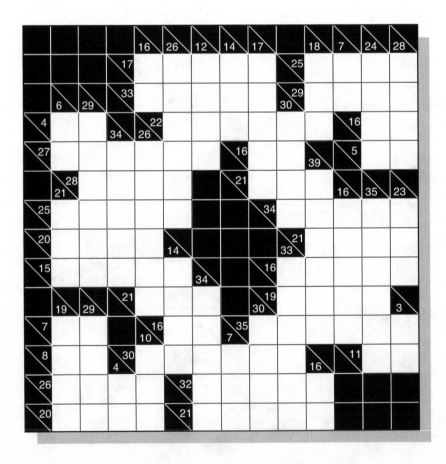

35

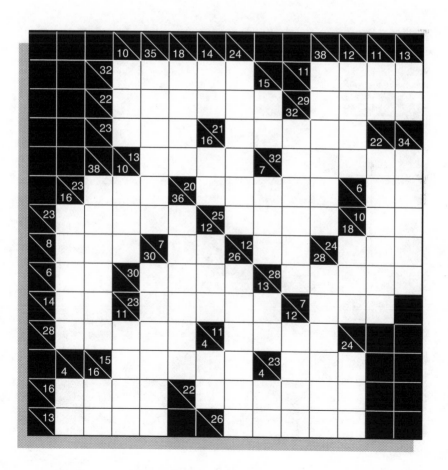

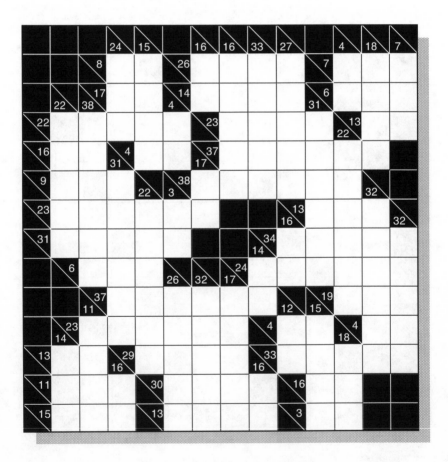

37

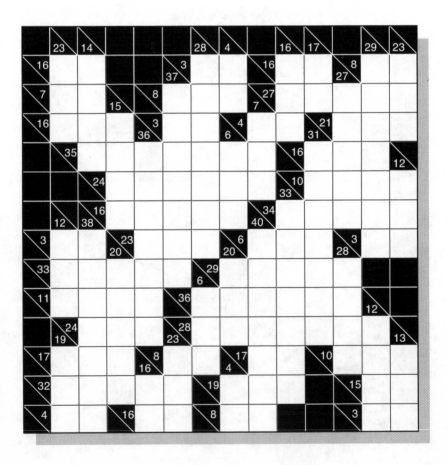

39

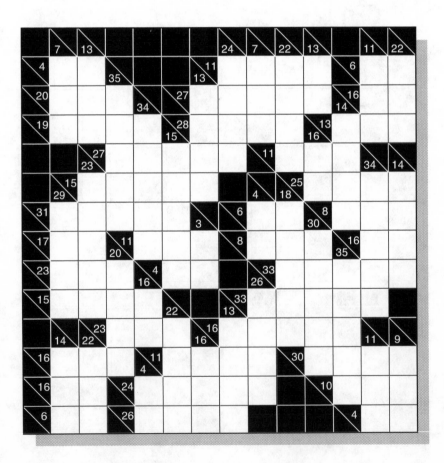

41

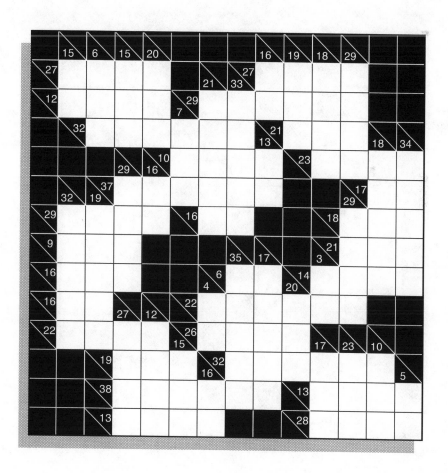

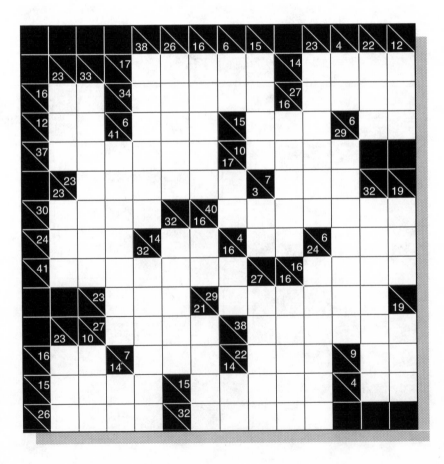

43

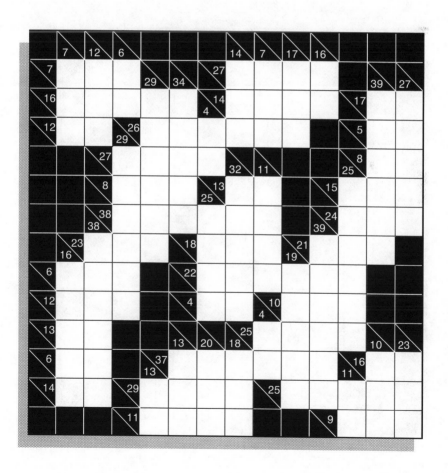

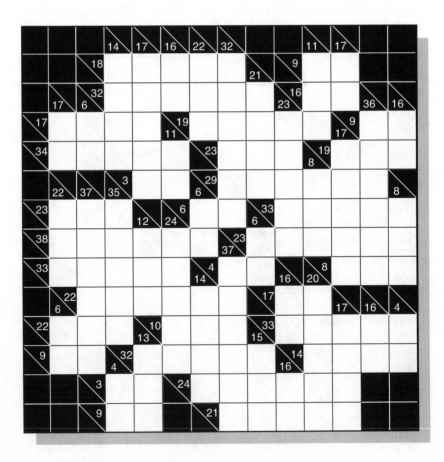

45

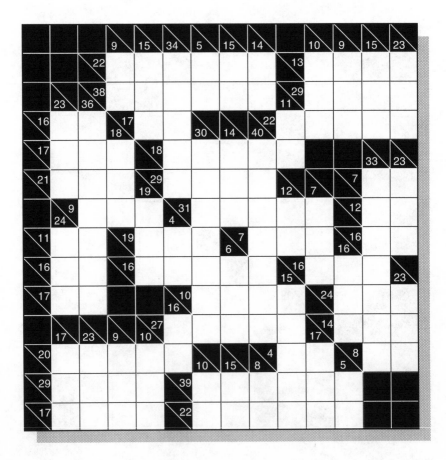

47

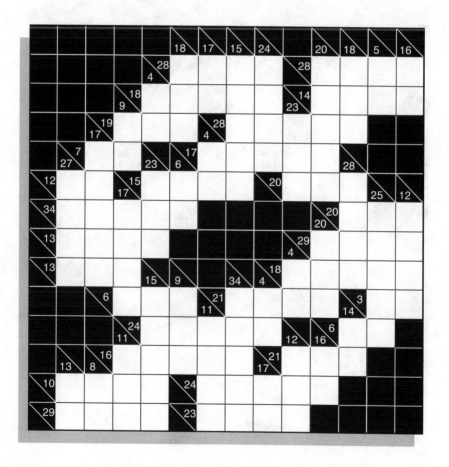

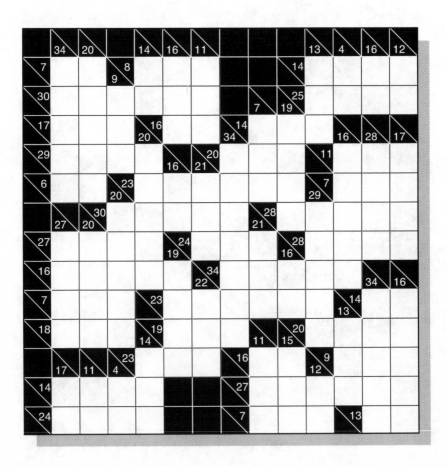

49

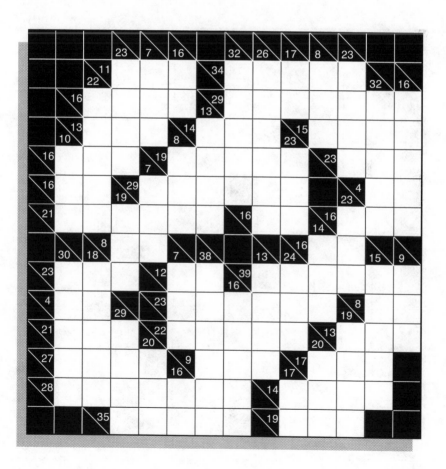

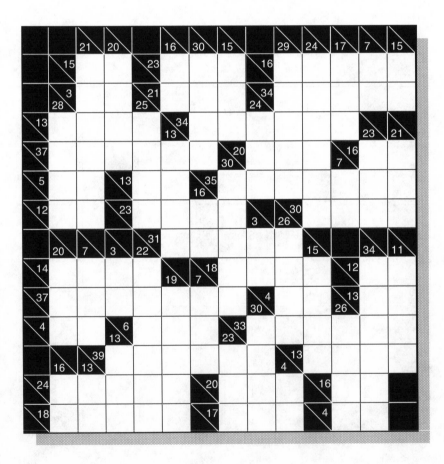

51

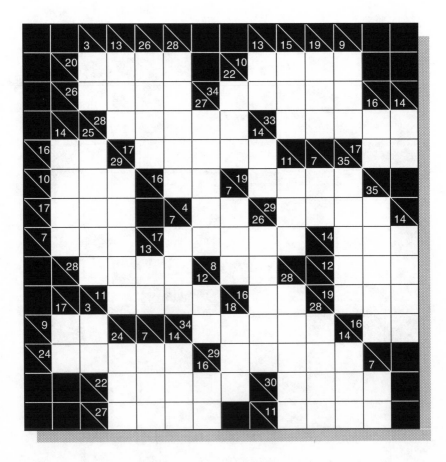

53

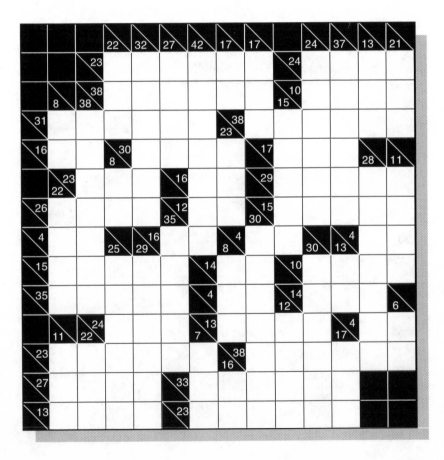

55

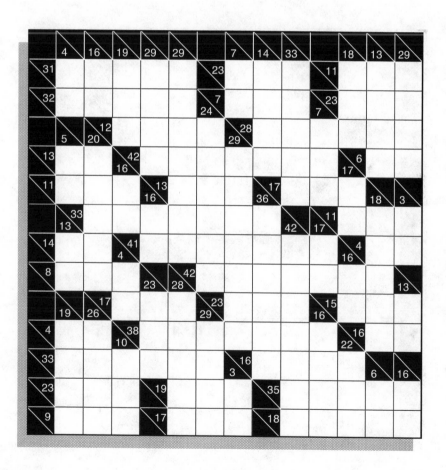

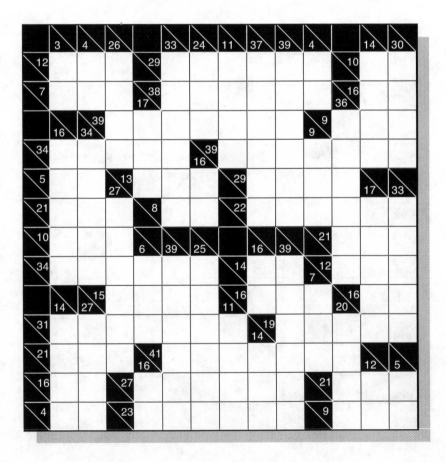

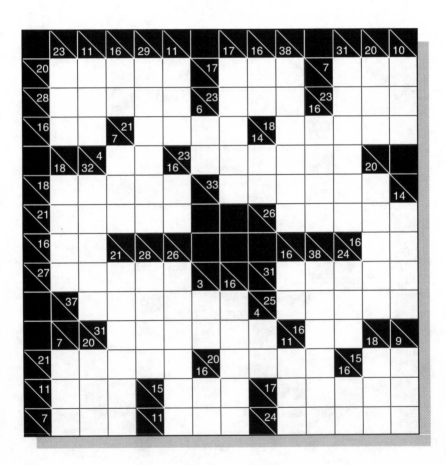

59

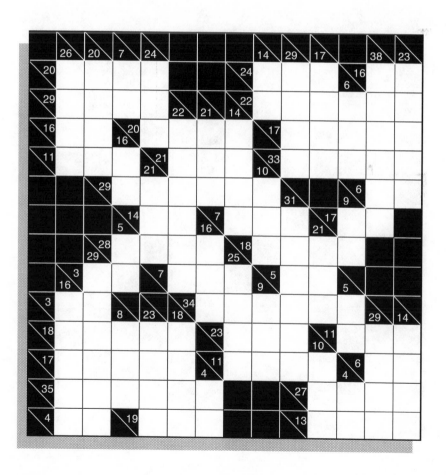

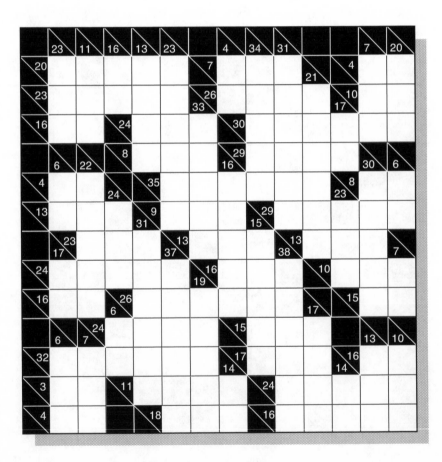

60

61

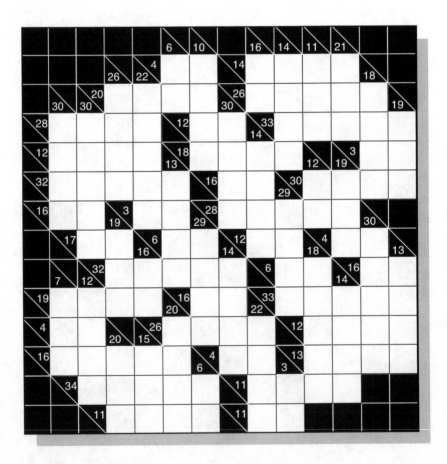

63

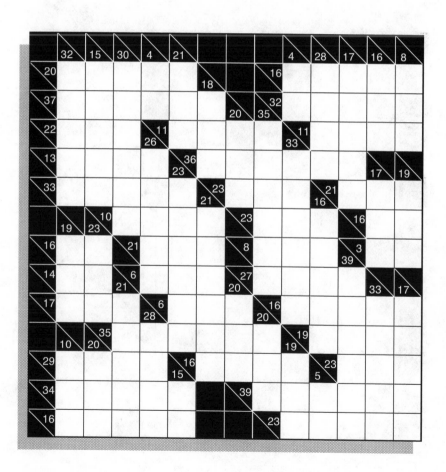

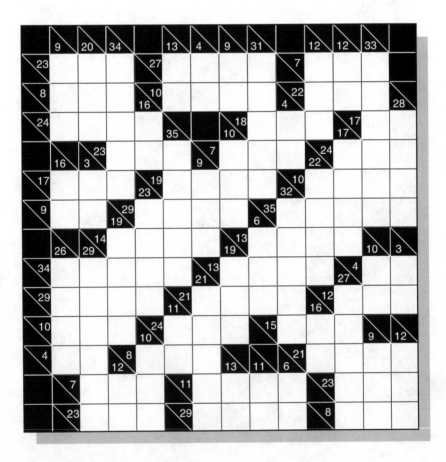

65

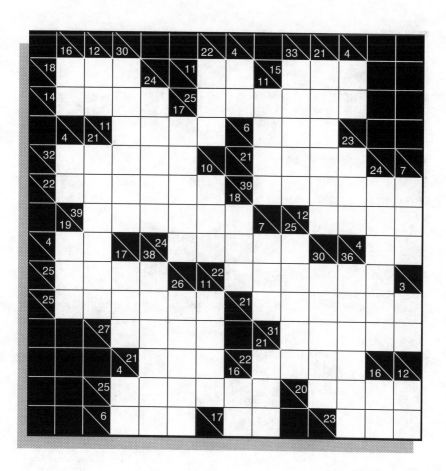

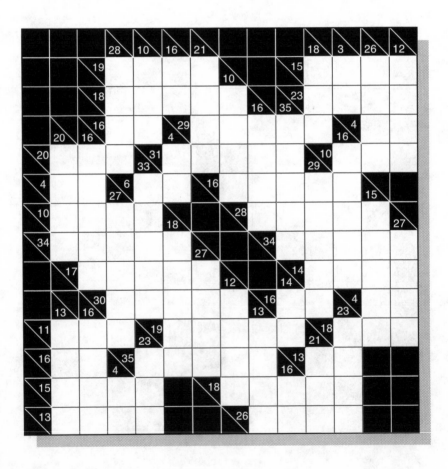

67

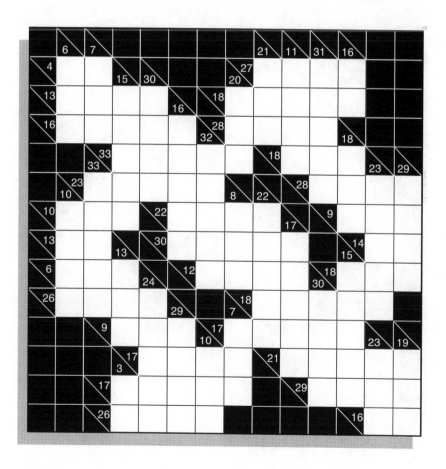

68

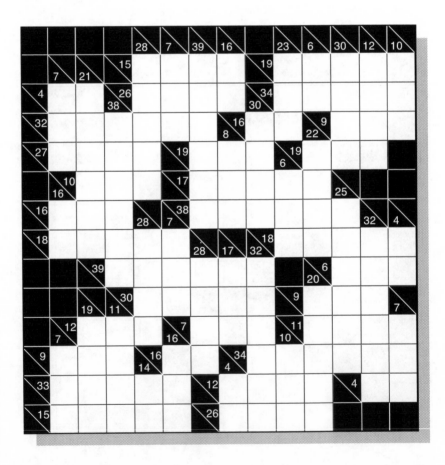

69

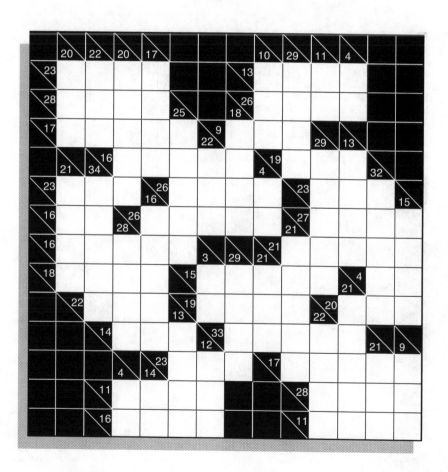

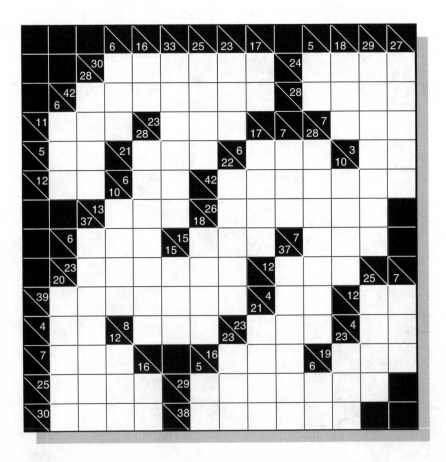

71

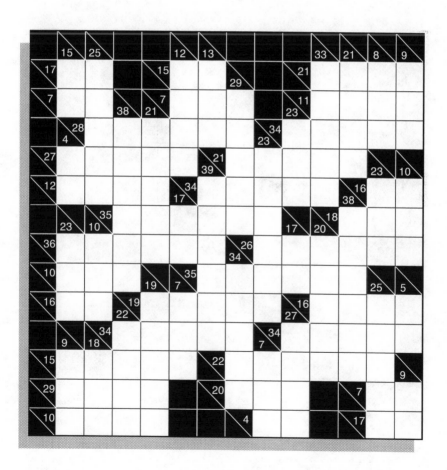

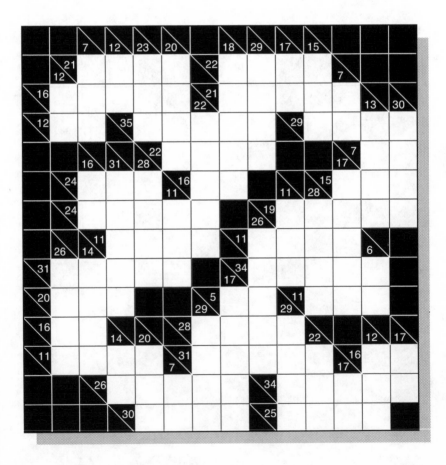

73

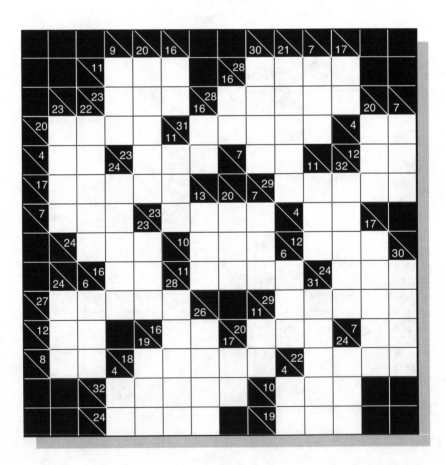

75

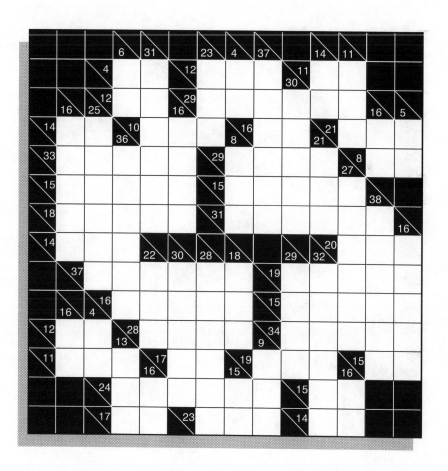

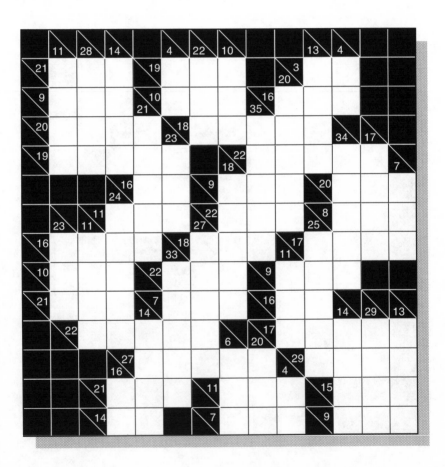

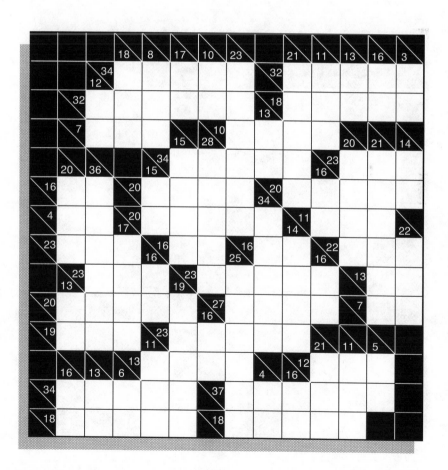

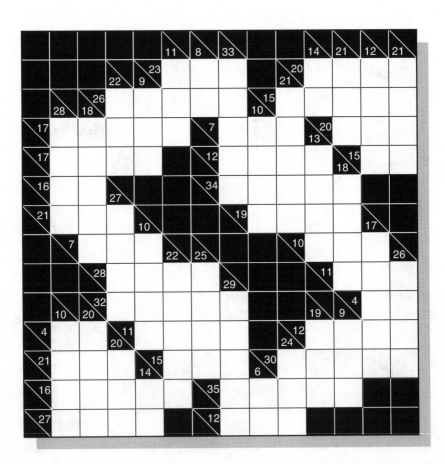

79

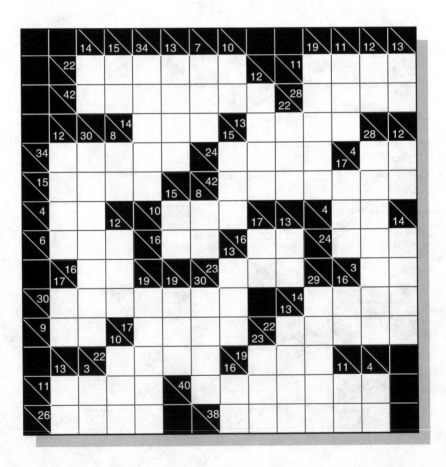

81

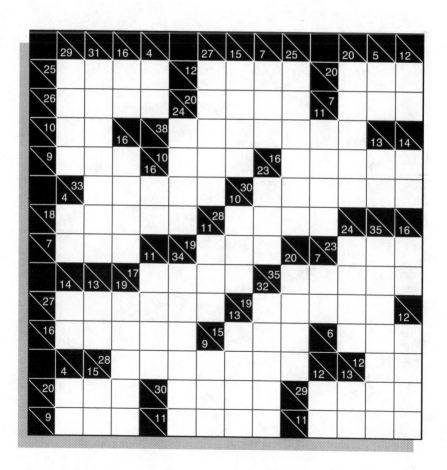

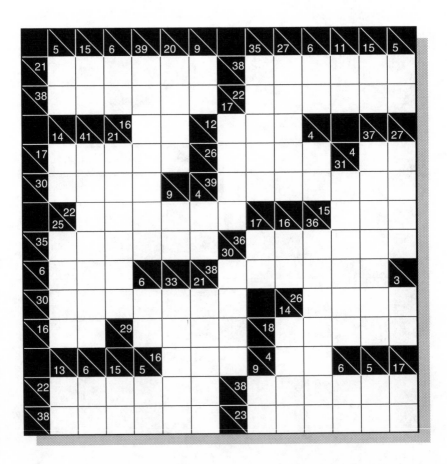

Part 3
Extremely Challenging Puzzles

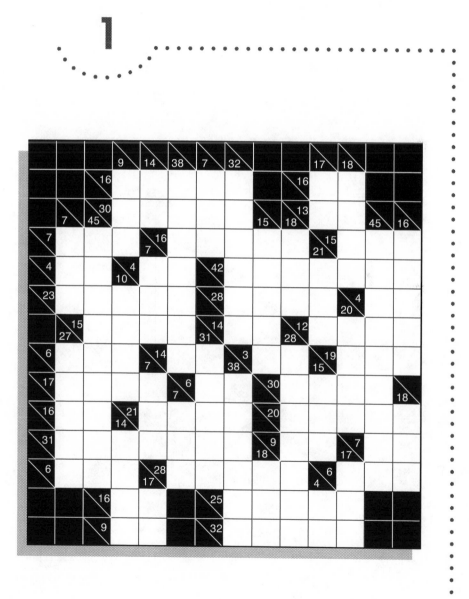

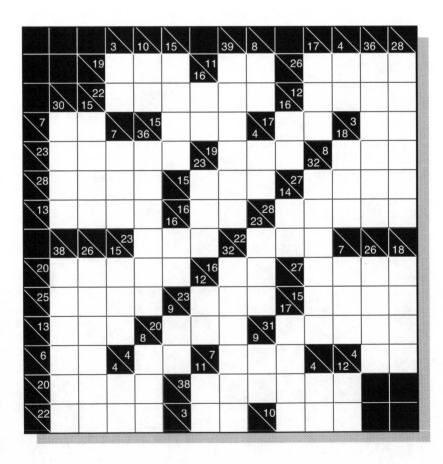

3

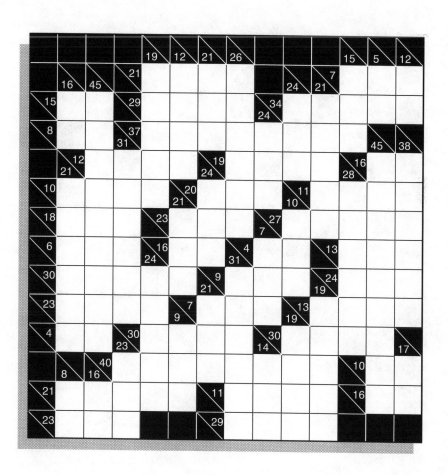

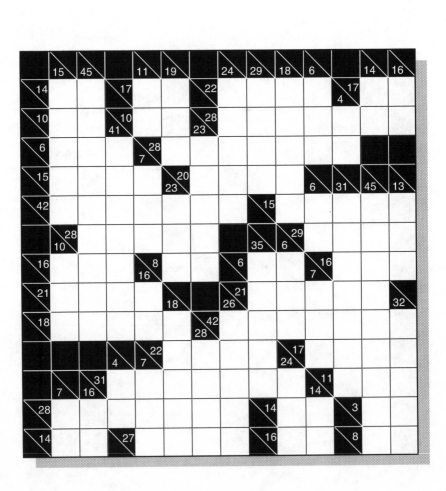

5

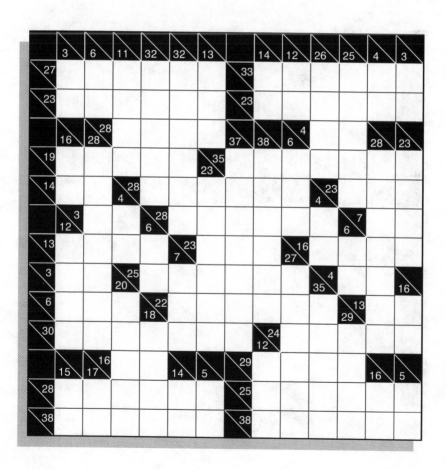

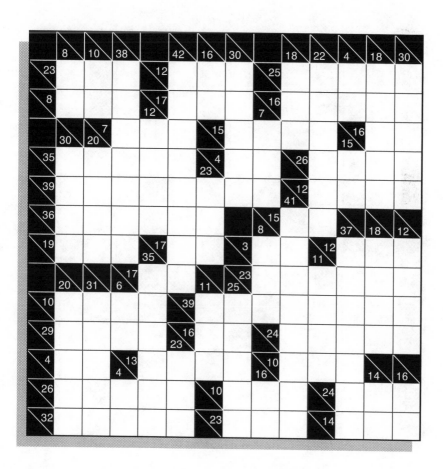

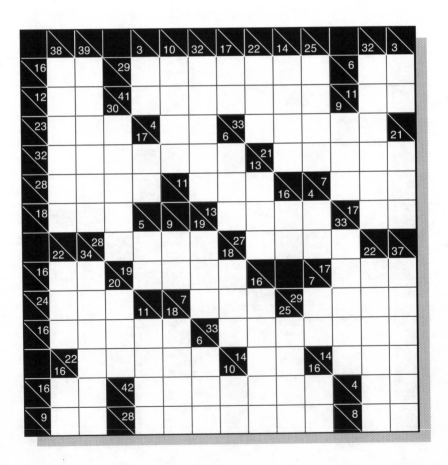

10

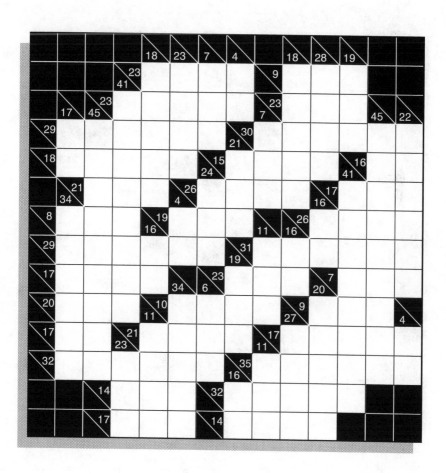

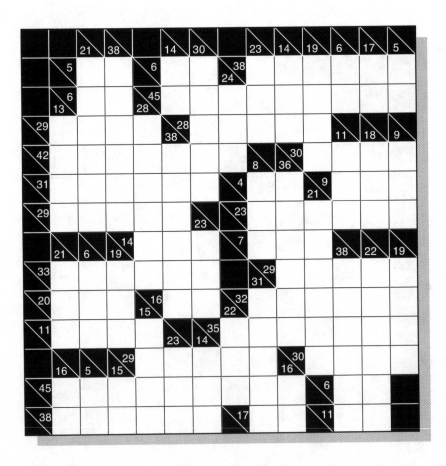

13

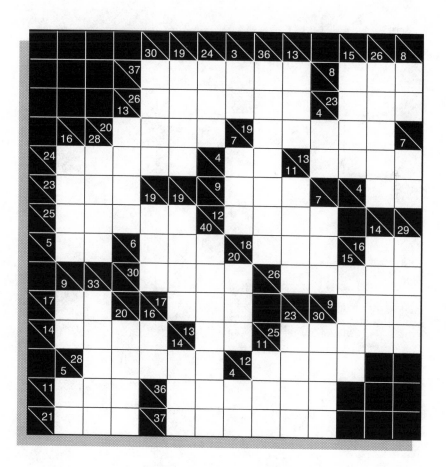

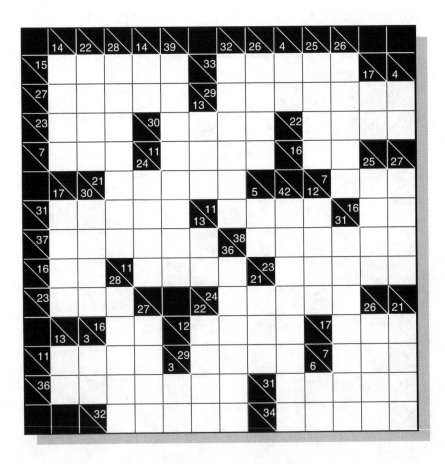

15

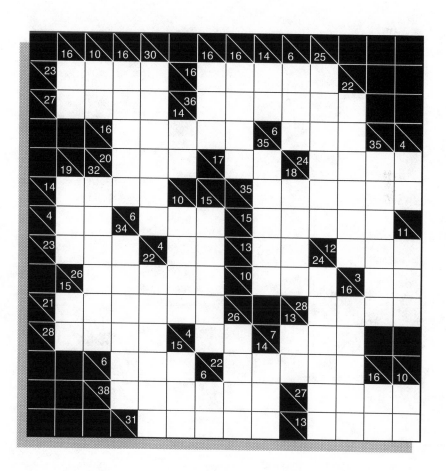

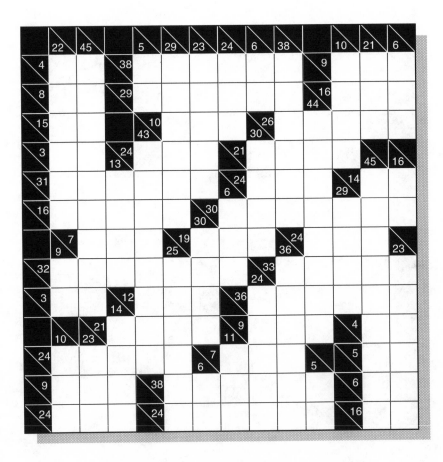

17

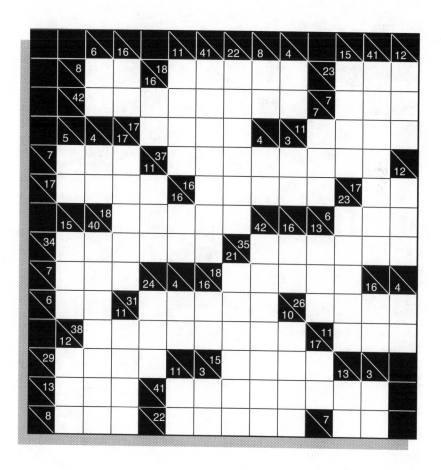

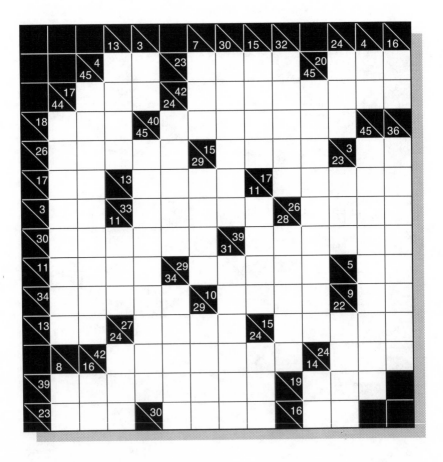

19

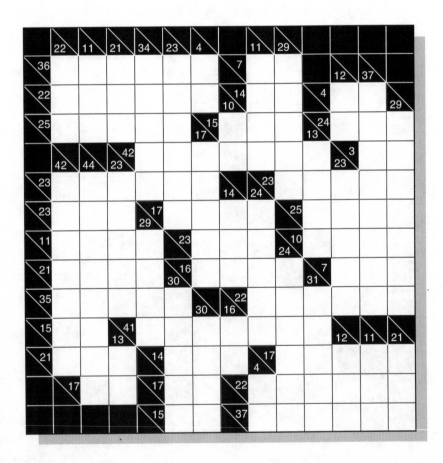

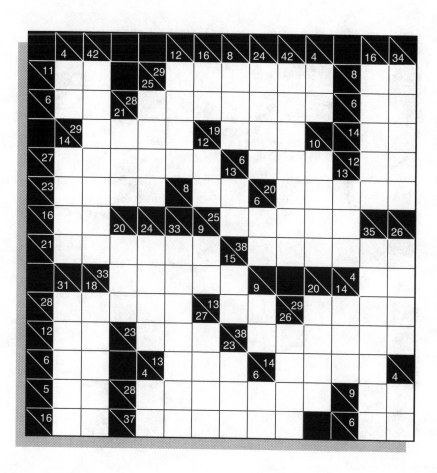

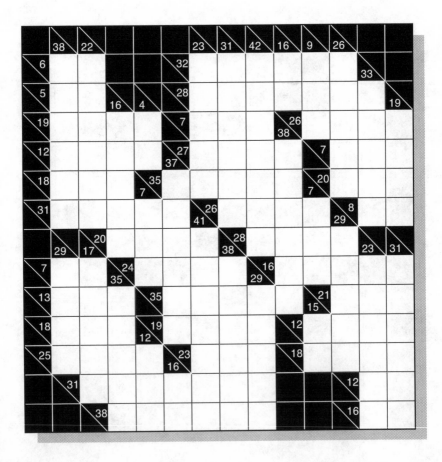

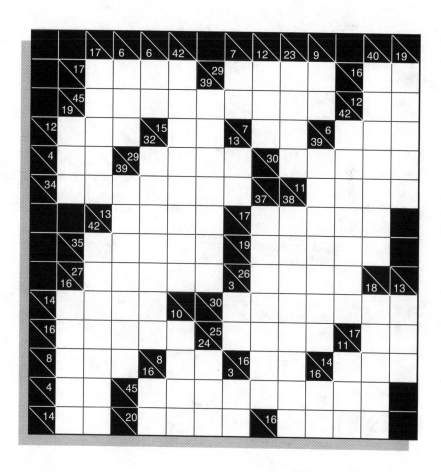

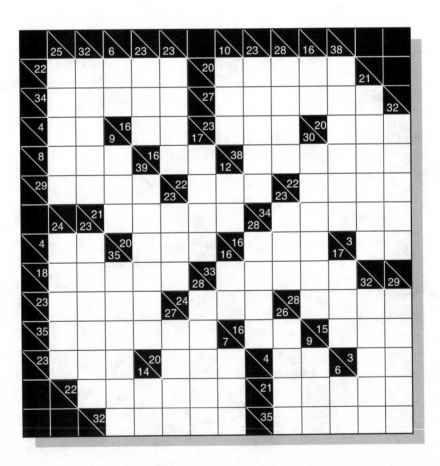

25

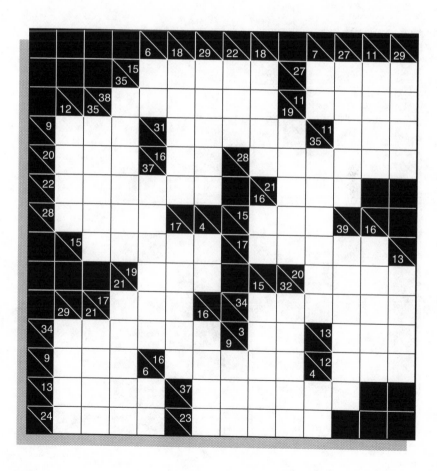

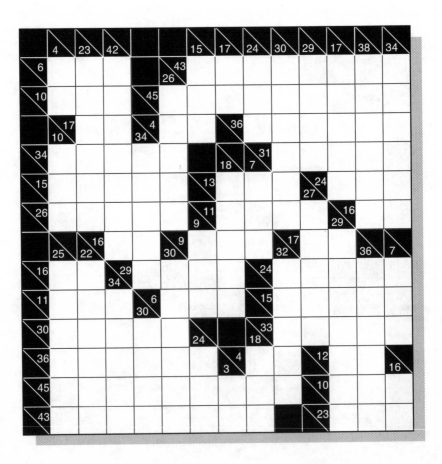

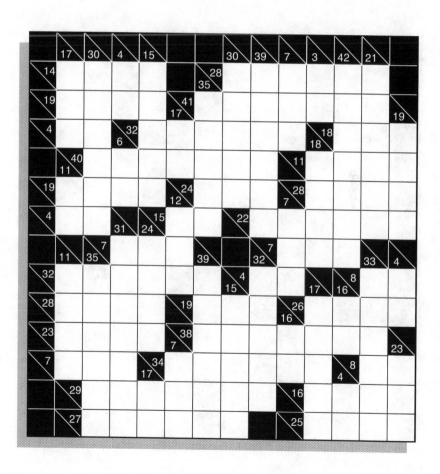

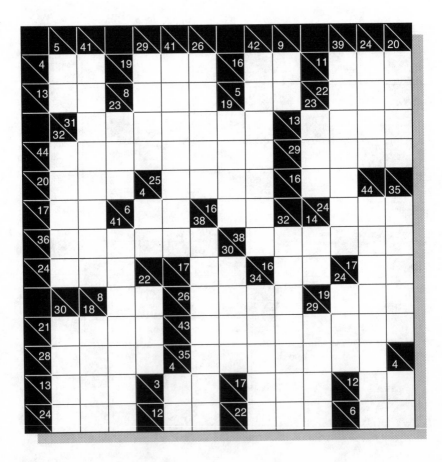

29

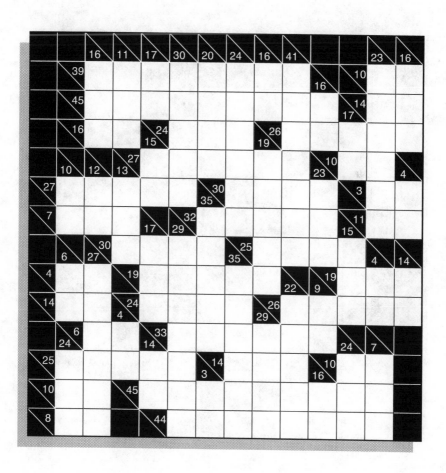

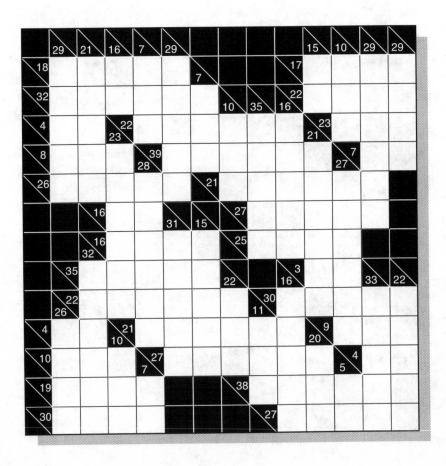

31

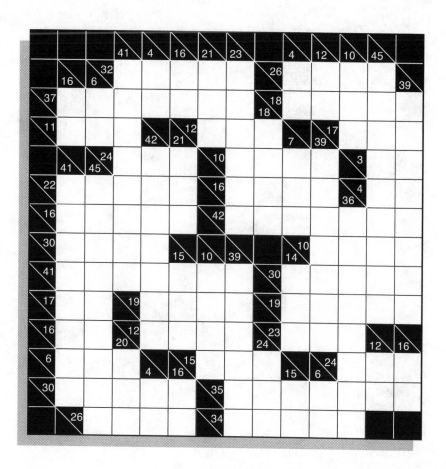

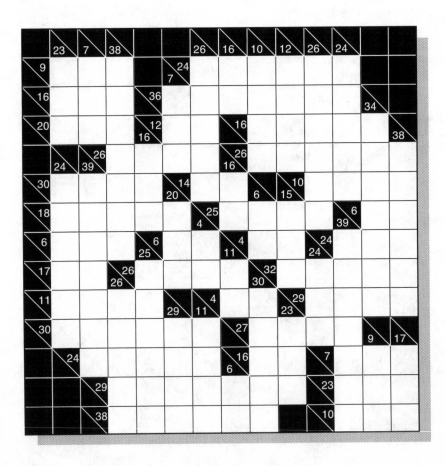

33

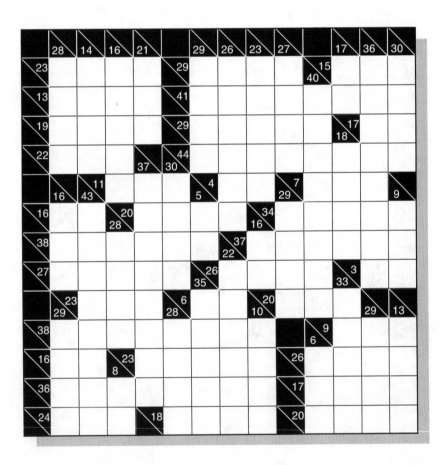

35

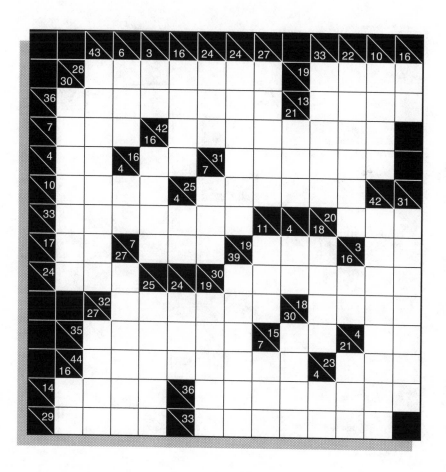

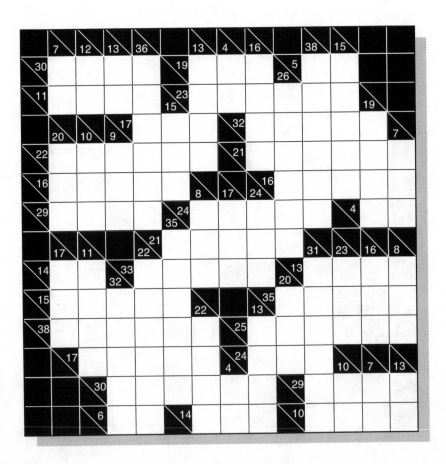

37

39

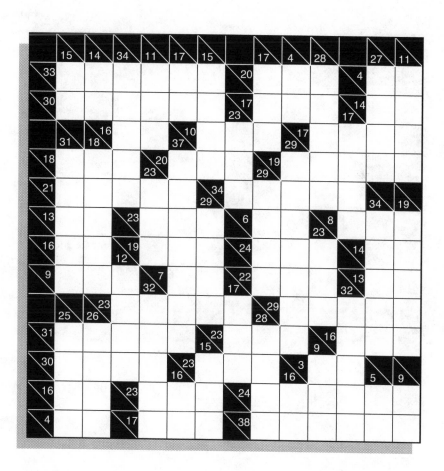

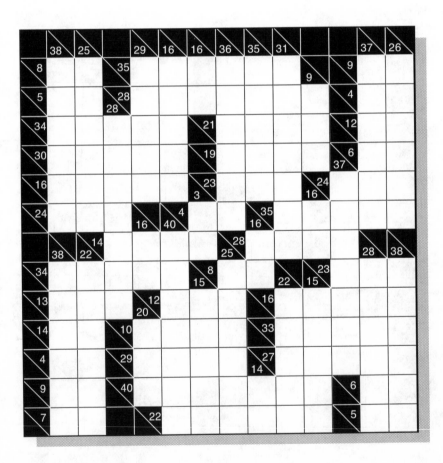

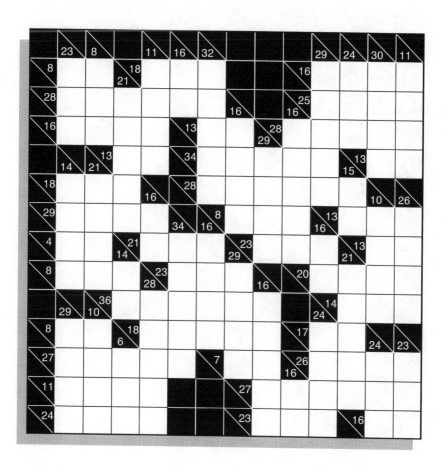

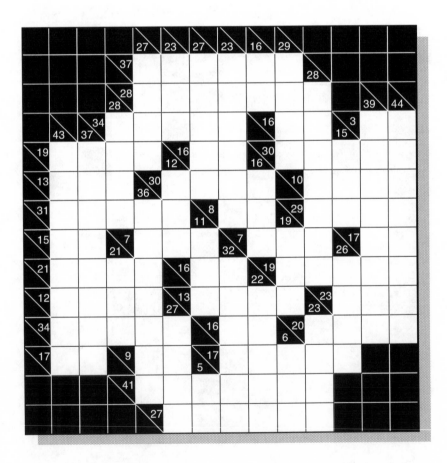

43

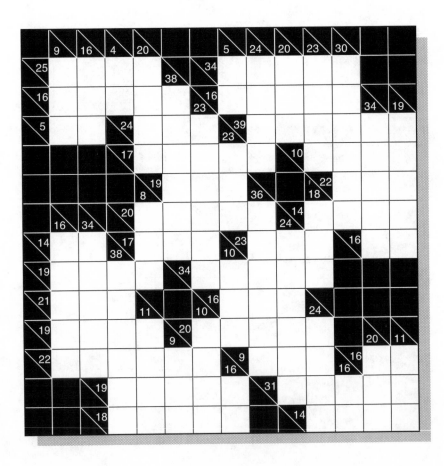

45

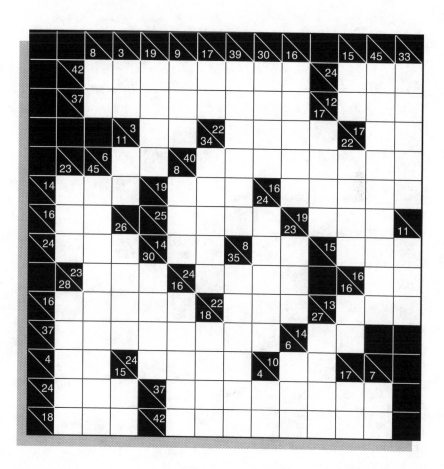

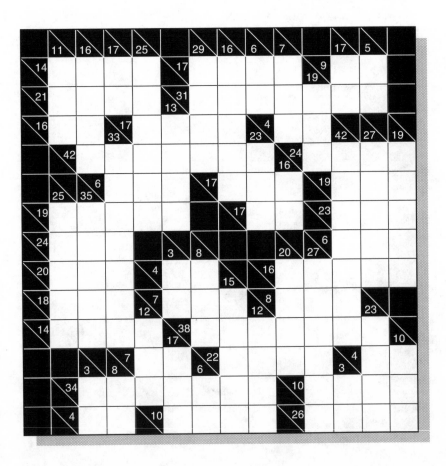

47

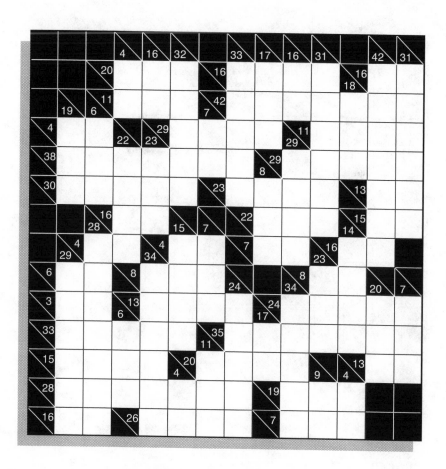

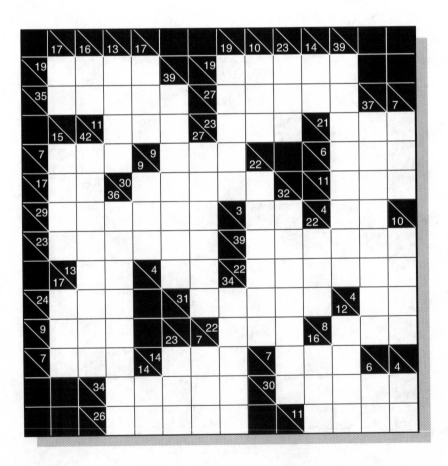

49

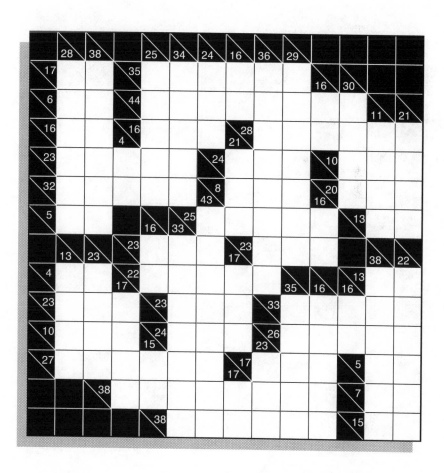

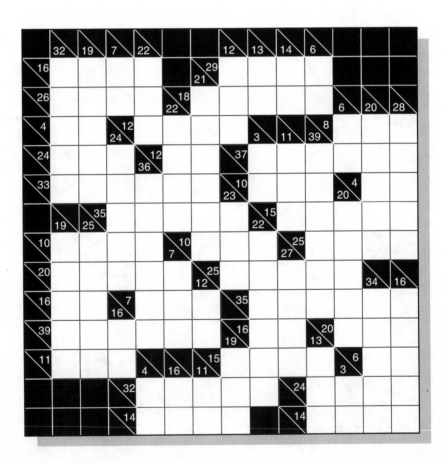

51

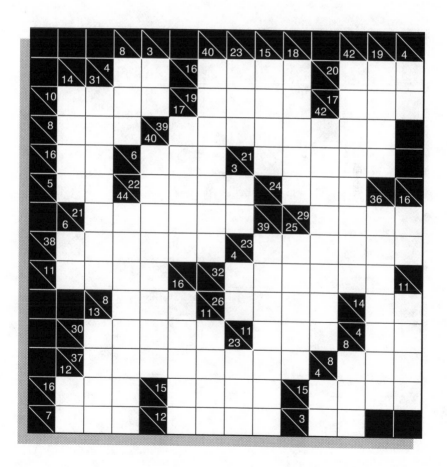

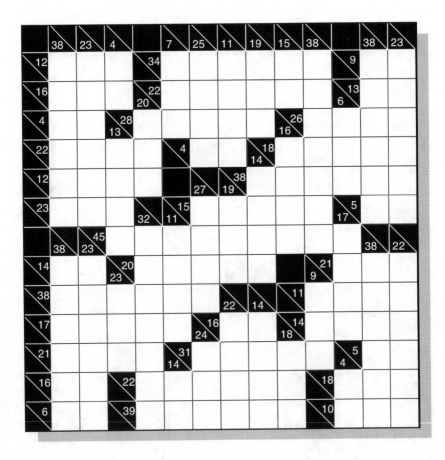

53

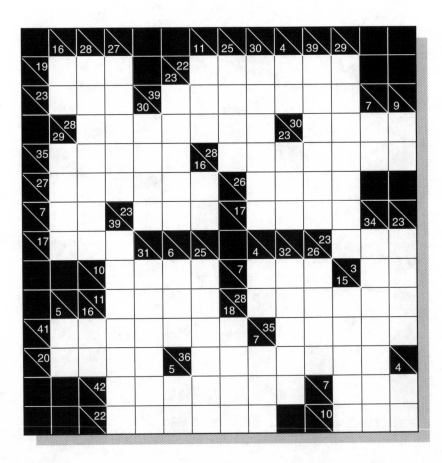

54

55

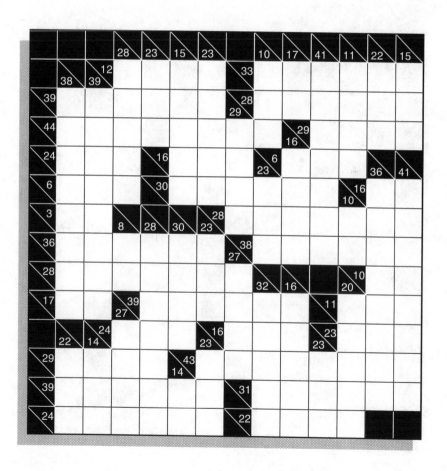

57

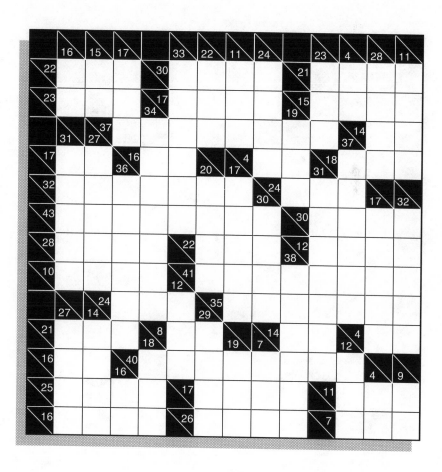

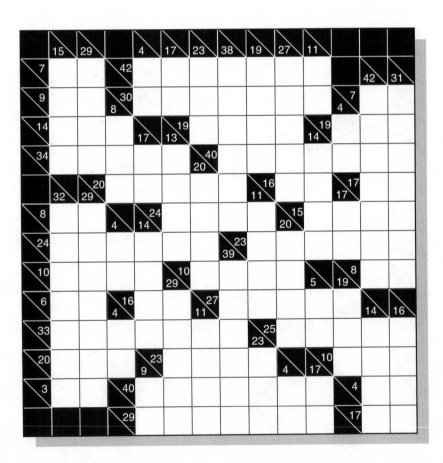

59

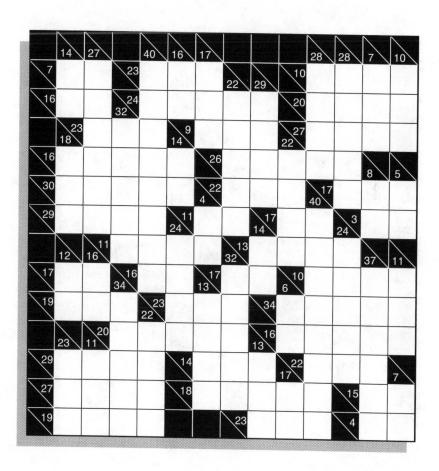

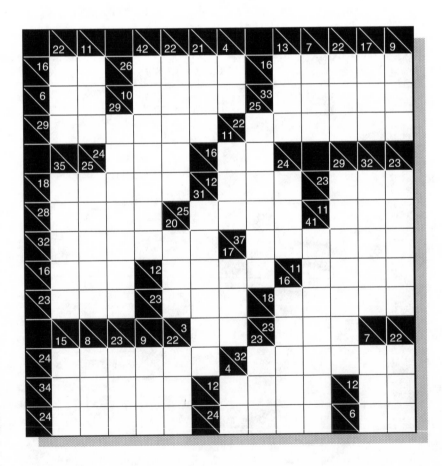

61

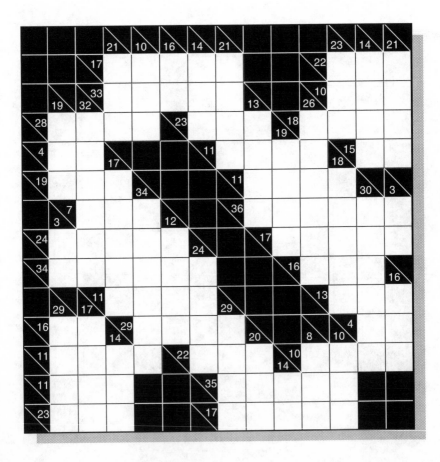

63

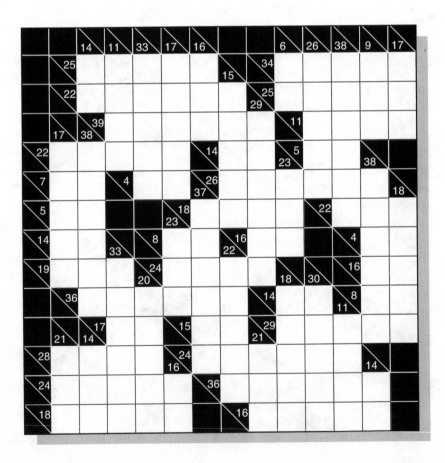

65

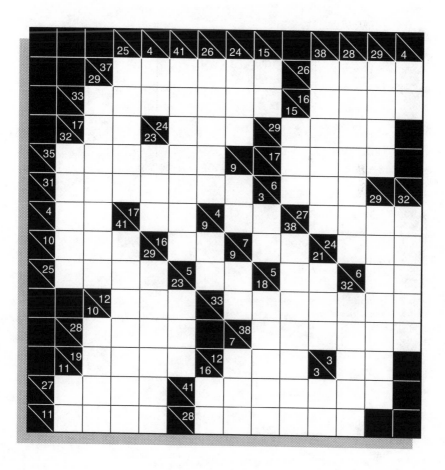

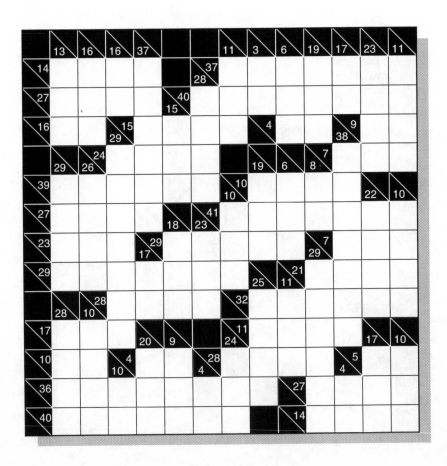

66

67

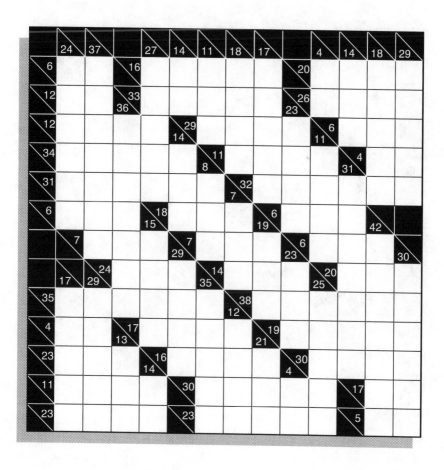

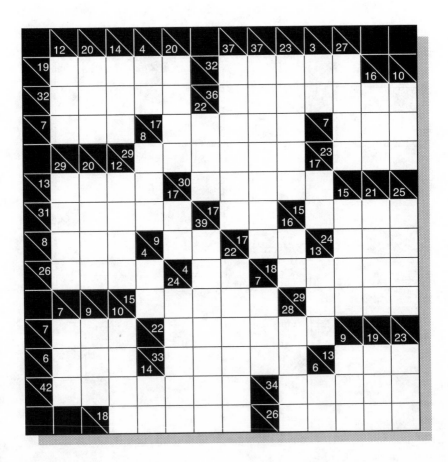

69

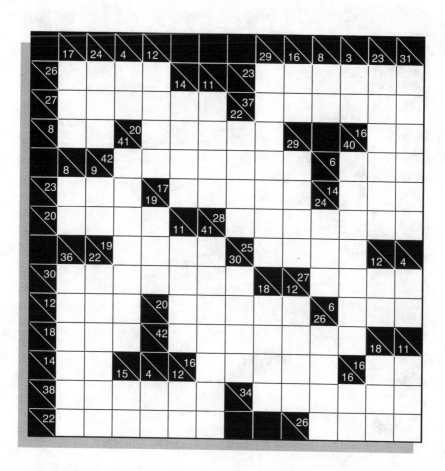

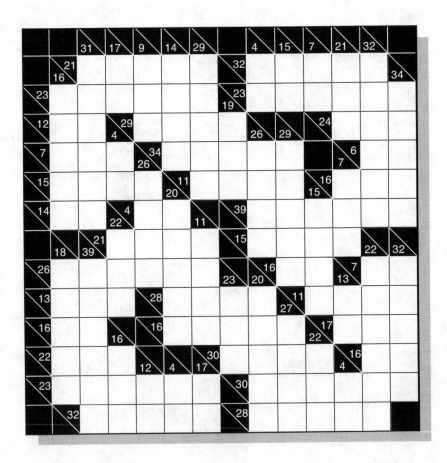

71

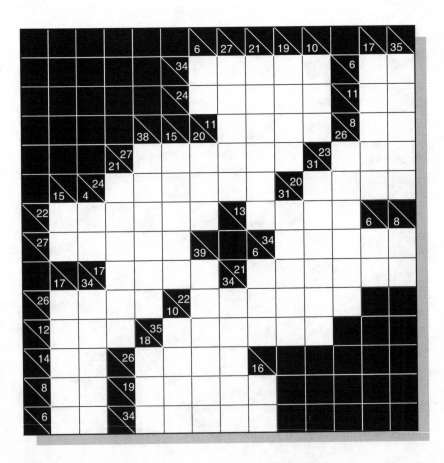

73

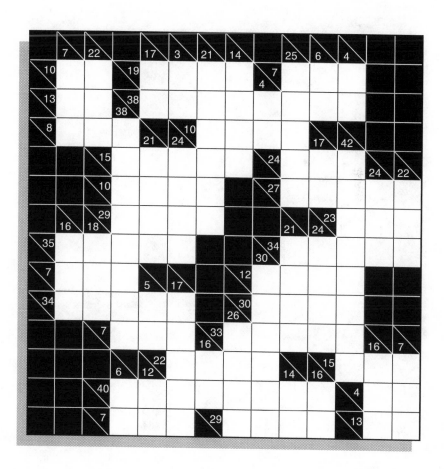

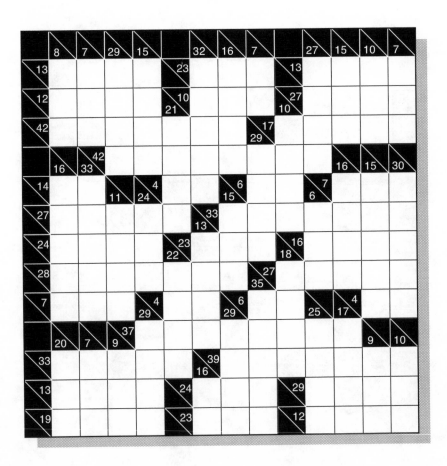

75

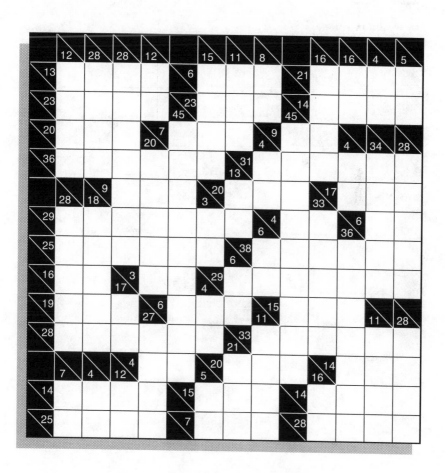

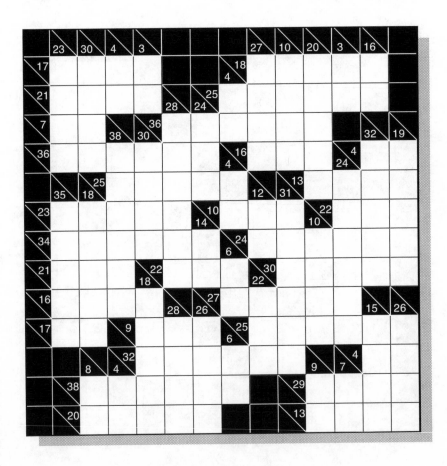

77

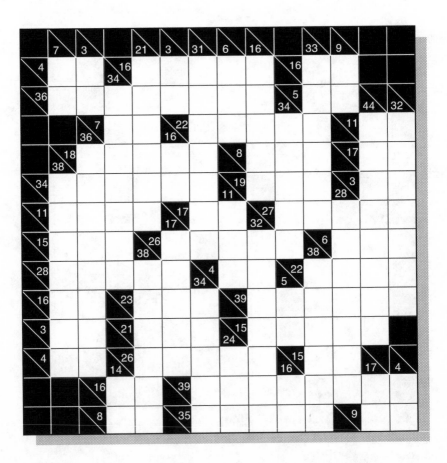

79

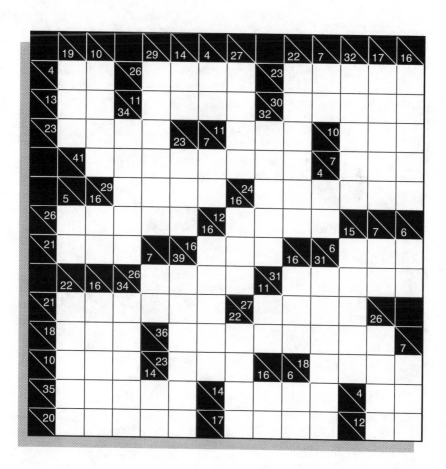

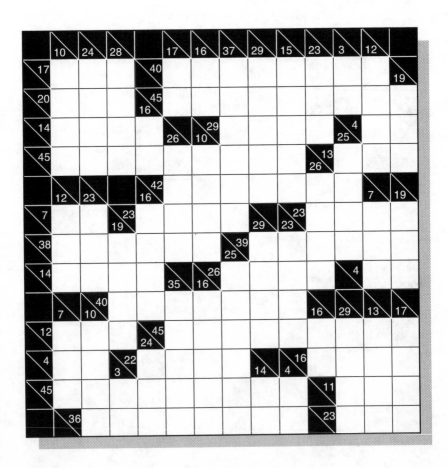

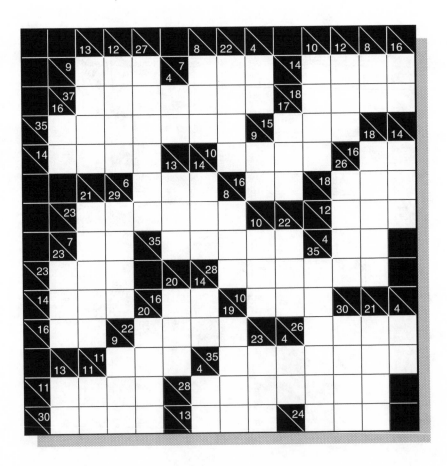

appendix a
Answers

Part 1: Mildly Challenging Puzzles

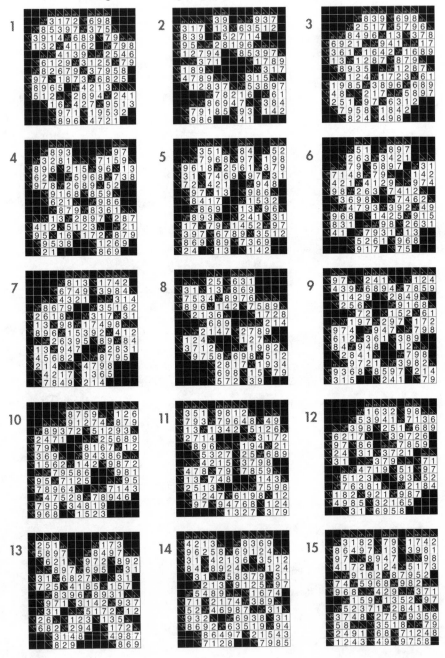

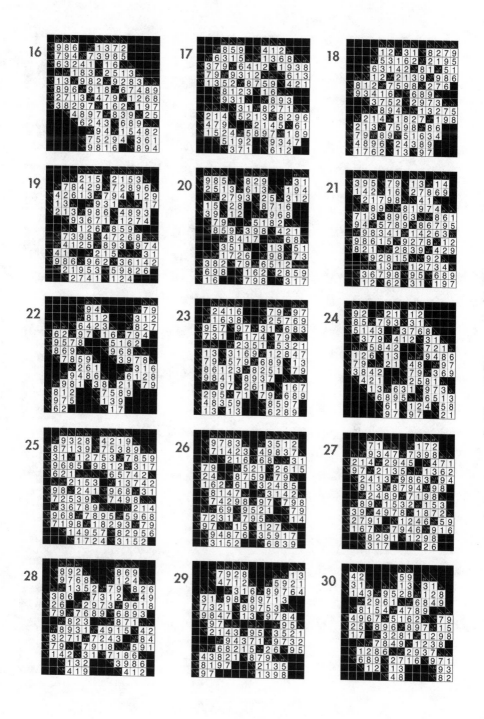

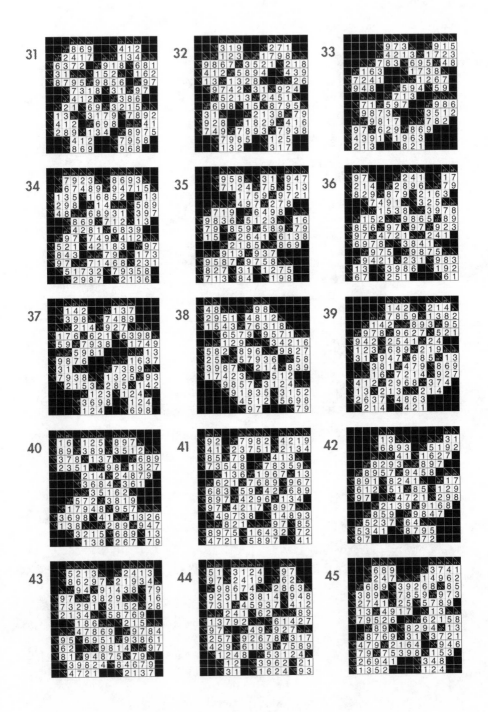

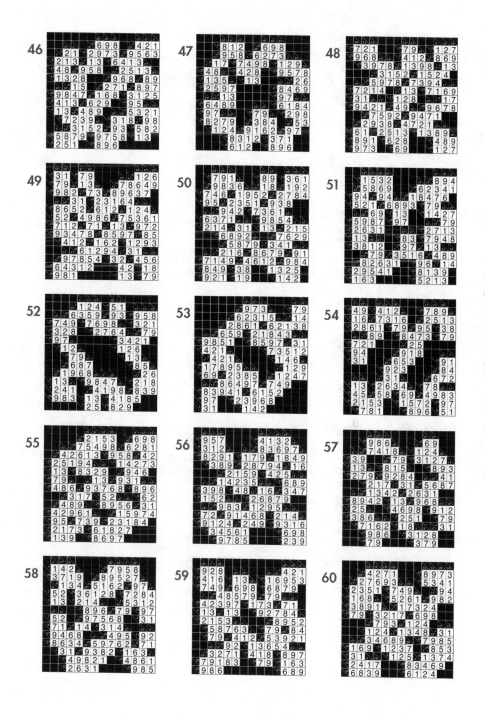

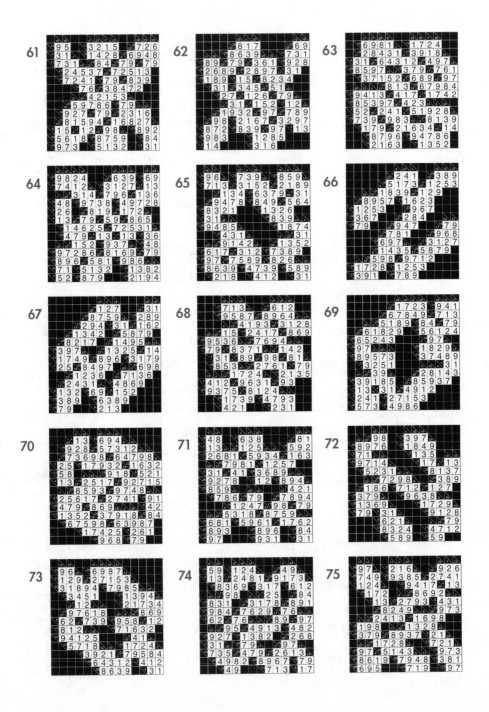

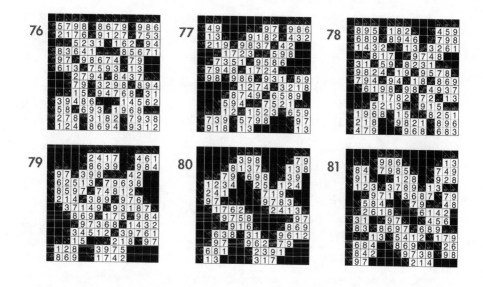

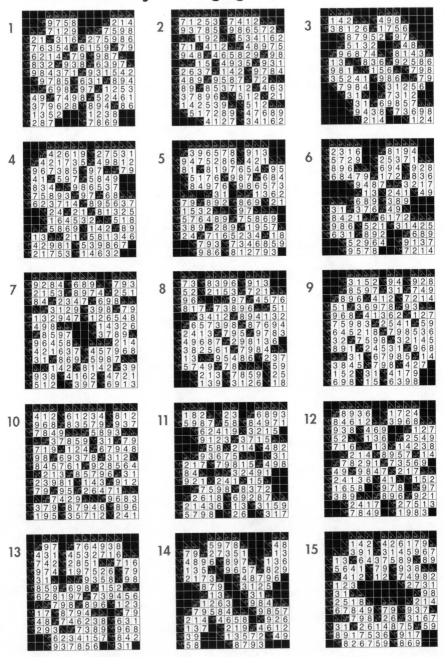

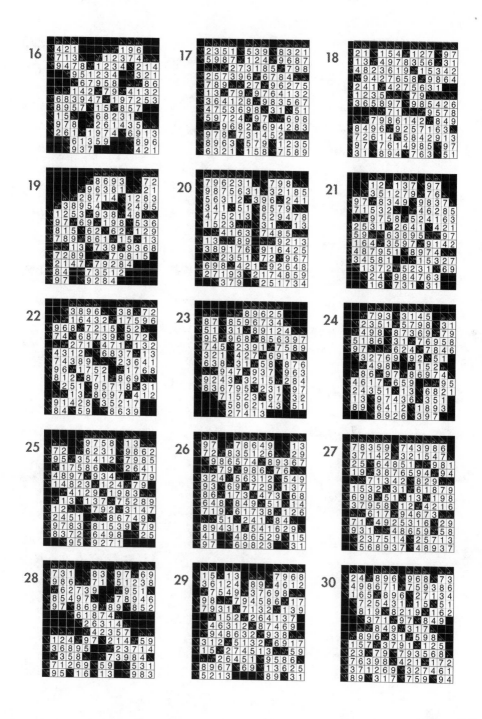

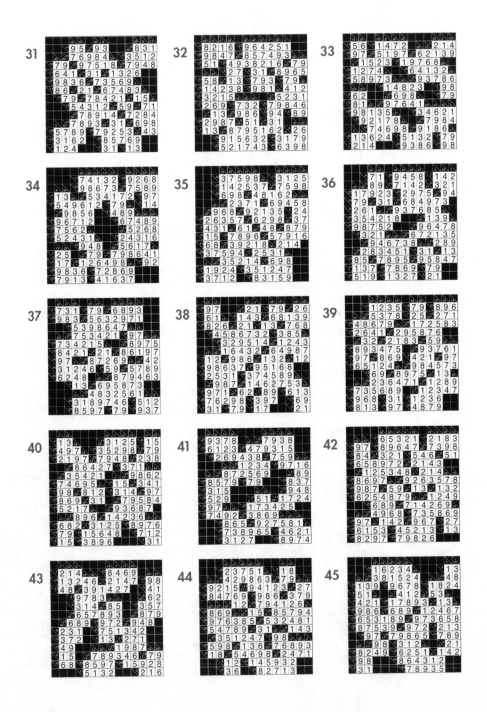

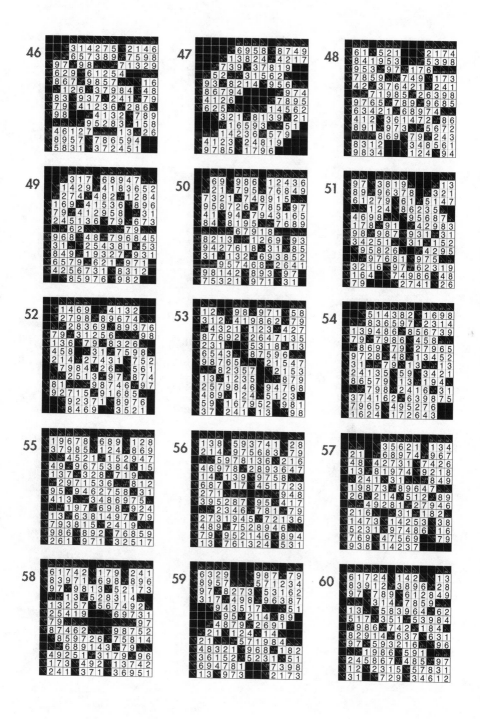

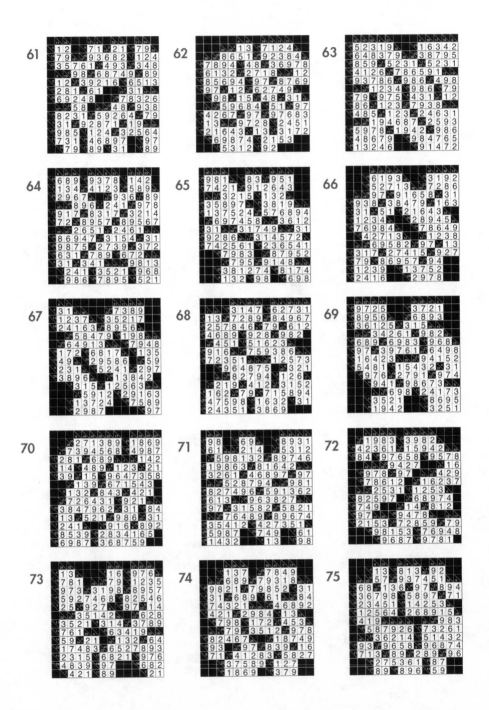

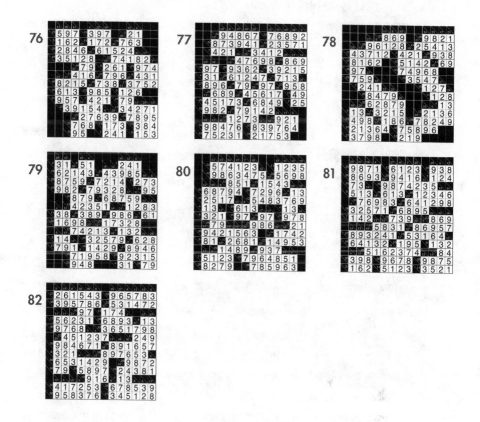

Part 3: Extremely Challenging Puzzles

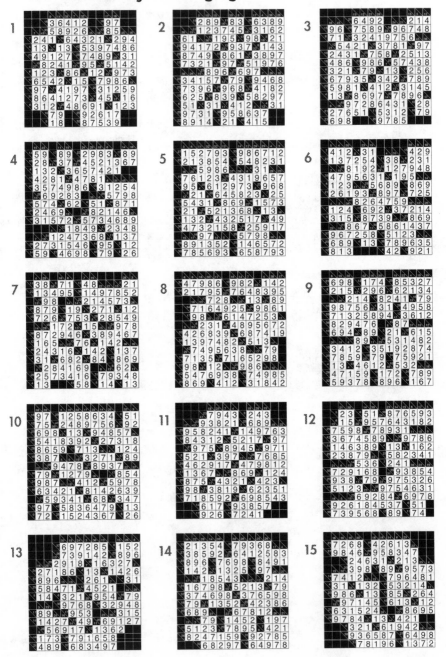

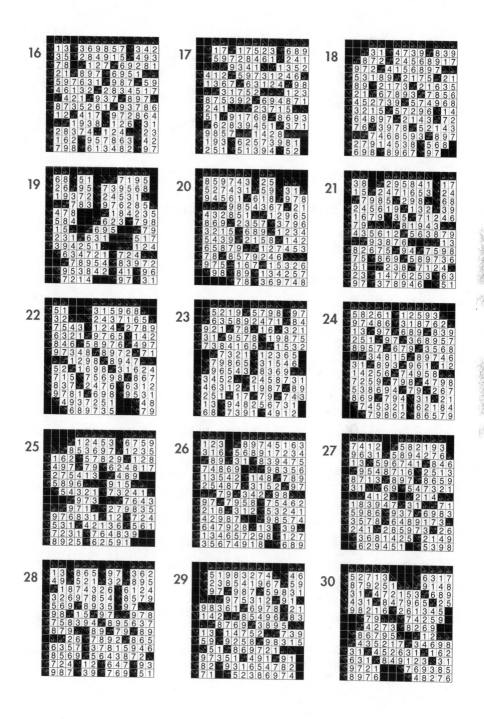

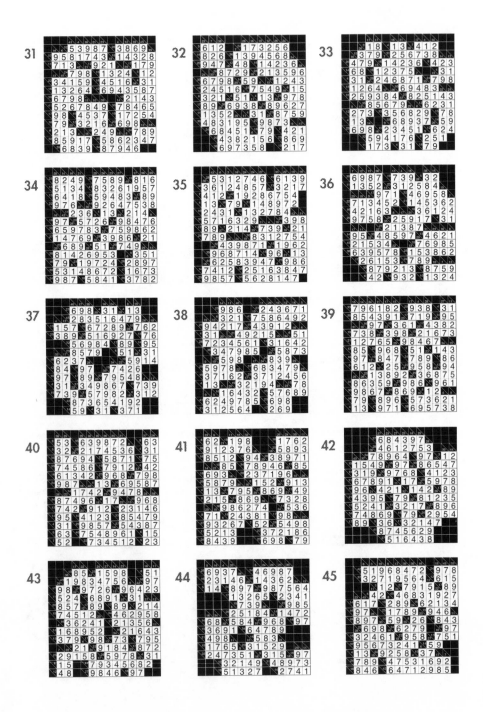

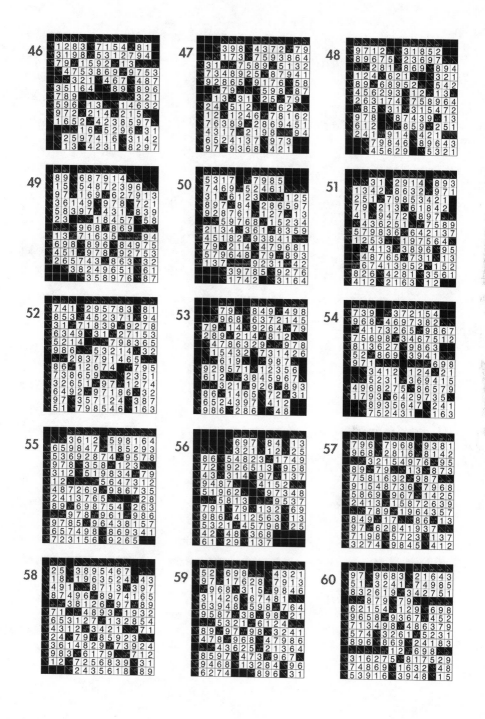

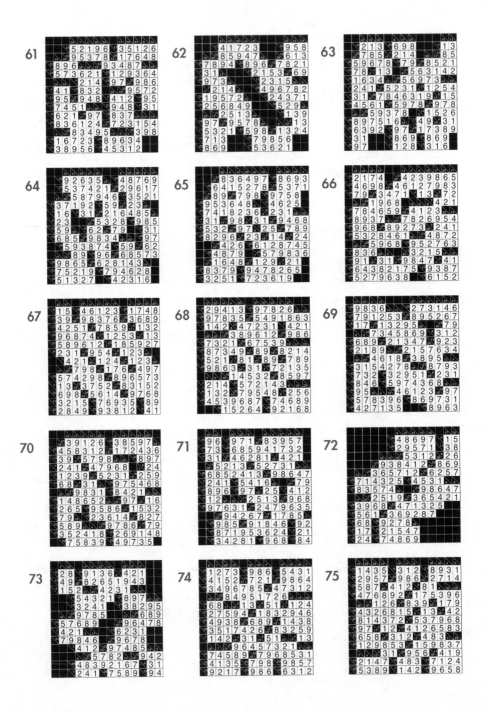

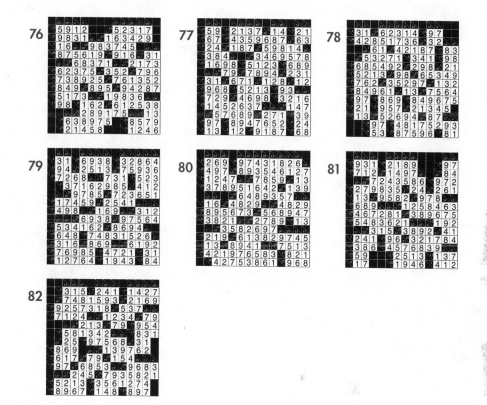

appendix b
Sum Combinations

Sum Combinations

number of spaces	sum	possible combinations
2	3	1, 2
2	4	1, 3
2	5	1, 4; 2, 3
2	6	1, 5; 2, 4
2	7	1, 6; 2, 5; 3, 4
2	8	1, 7; 2, 6; 3, 5
2	9	1, 8; 2, 7; 3, 6; 4, 5
2	10	1, 9; 2, 8; 3, 7; 4, 6
2	11	2, 9; 3, 8; 4, 7; 5, 6
2	12	3, 9; 4, 8; 5, 7
2	13	4, 9; 5, 8; 6, 7
2	14	5, 9; 6, 8
2	15	6, 9; 7, 8
2	16	7, 9
2	17	8, 9
3	6	1, 2, 3
3	7	1, 2, 4
3	8	1, 2, 5; 1, 3, 4
3	9	1, 2, 6; 1, 3, 5; 2, 3, 4
3	10	1, 2, 7; 1, 3, 6; 1, 4, 5; 2, 3, 5
3	11	1, 2, 8; 1, 3, 7; 1, 4, 6; 2, 3, 6; 2, 4, 5
3	12	1, 2, 9; 1, 3, 8; 1, 4, 7; 1, 5, 6; 2, 3, 7; 2, 4, 6; 3, 4, 5
3	13	1, 3, 9; 1, 4, 8; 1, 5, 7; 2, 3, 8; 2, 4, 7; 2, 5, 6; 3, 4, 6
3	14	1, 4, 9; 1, 5, 8; 1, 6, 7; 2, 3, 9; 2, 4, 8; 2, 5, 7; 3, 4, 7; 3, 5, 6
3	15	1, 5, 9; 1, 6, 8; 2, 4, 9; 2, 5, 8; 2, 6, 7; 3, 4, 8; 3, 5, 7; 4, 5, 6
3	16	1, 6, 9; 1, 7, 8; 2, 5, 9; 2, 6, 8; 3, 4, 9; 3, 5, 8; 3, 6, 7; 4, 5, 7

3	17	1, 7, 9; 2, 6, 9; 2, 7, 8; 3, 5, 9; 3, 6, 8; 4, 5, 8; 4, 6, 7
3	18	1, 8, 9; 2, 7, 9; 3, 6, 9; 3, 7, 8; 4, 5, 9; 4, 6, 8; 5, 6, 7
3	19	2, 8, 9; 3, 7, 9; 4, 6, 9; 4, 7, 8; 5, 6, 8
3	20	3, 8, 9; 4, 7, 9; 5, 6, 9; 5, 7, 8
3	21	4, 8, 9; 5, 7, 9; 6, 7, 8
3	22	5, 8, 9; 6, 7, 9
3	23	6, 8, 9
3	24	7, 8, 9
4	10	1, 2, 3, 4
4	11	1, 2, 3, 5
4	12	1, 2, 3, 6; 1, 2, 4, 5
4	13	1, 2, 3, 7; 1, 2, 4, 6; 1, 3, 4, 5
4	14	1, 2, 3, 8; 1, 2, 4, 7; 1, 2, 5, 6; 1, 3, 4, 6; 2, 3, 4, 5
4	15	1, 2, 3, 9; 1, 2, 4, 8; 1, 2, 5, 7; 1, 3, 4, 7; 1, 3, 5, 6; 2, 3, 4, 6
4	16	1, 2, 4, 9; 1, 2, 5, 8; 1, 2, 6, 7; 1, 3, 4, 8; 1, 3, 5, 7; 1, 4, 5, 6; 2, 3, 4, 7; 2, 3, 5, 6
4	17	1, 2, 5, 9; 1, 2, 6, 8; 1, 3, 4, 9; 1, 3, 5, 8; 1, 3, 6, 7; 1, 4, 5, 7; 2, 3, 4, 8; 2, 3, 5, 7; 2, 4, 5, 6
4	18	1, 2, 6, 9; 1, 2, 7, 8; 1, 3, 5, 9; 1, 3, 6, 8; 1, 4, 5, 8; 1, 4, 6, 7; 2, 3, 4, 9; 2, 3, 5, 8; 2, 3, 6, 7; 2, 4, 5, 7; 3, 4, 5, 6
4	19	1, 2, 7, 9; 1, 3, 6, 9; 1, 3, 7, 8; 1, 4, 5, 9; 1, 4, 6, 8; 1, 5, 6, 7; 2, 3, 5, 9; 2, 3, 6, 8; 2, 4, 5, 8; 2, 4, 6, 7; 3, 4, 5, 7
4	20	1, 2, 8, 9; 1, 3, 7, 9; 1, 4, 6, 9; 1, 4, 7, 8; 1, 5, 6, 8; 2, 3, 6, 9; 2, 3, 7, 8; 2, 4, 5, 9; 2, 4, 6, 8; 2, 5, 6, 7; 3, 4, 5, 8; 3, 4, 6, 7
4	21	1, 3, 8, 9; 1, 4, 7, 9; 1, 5, 6, 9; 1, 5, 7, 8; 2, 3, 7, 9; 2, 4, 6, 9; 2, 4, 7, 8; 2, 5, 6, 8; 3, 4, 5, 9; 3, 4, 6, 8; 3, 5, 6, 7
4	22	1, 4, 8, 9; 1, 5, 7, 9; 1, 6, 7, 8; 2, 3, 8, 9; 2, 4, 7, 9; 2, 5, 6, 9; 2, 5, 7, 8; 3, 4, 6, 9; 3, 4, 7, 8; 3, 5, 6, 8; 4, 5, 6, 7

4	23	1, 5, 8, 9; 1, 6, 7, 9; 2, 4, 8, 9; 2, 5, 7, 9; 2, 6, 7, 8; 3, 4, 7, 9; 3, 5, 6, 9; 3, 5, 7, 8; 4, 5, 6, 8
4	24	1, 6, 8, 9; 2, 5, 8, 9; 2, 6, 7, 9; 3, 4, 8, 9; 3, 5, 7, 9; 3, 6, 7, 8; 4, 5, 6, 9; 4, 5, 7, 8
4	25	1, 7, 8, 9; 2, 6, 8, 9; 3, 5, 8, 9; 3, 6, 7, 9; 4, 5, 7, 9; 4, 6, 7, 8
4	26	2, 7, 8, 9; 3, 6, 8, 9; 4, 5, 8, 9; 4, 6, 7, 9; 5, 6, 7, 8
4	27	3, 7, 8, 9; 4, 6, 8, 9; 5, 6, 7, 9
4	28	4, 7, 8, 9; 5, 6, 8, 9
4	29	5, 7, 8, 9
4	30	6, 7, 8, 9
5	15	1, 2, 3, 4, 5
5	16	1, 2, 3, 4, 6
5	17	1, 2, 3, 4, 7; 1, 2, 3, 5, 6
5	18	1, 2, 3, 4, 8; 1, 2, 3, 5, 7; 1, 2, 4, 5, 6
5	19	1, 2, 3, 4, 9; 1, 2, 3, 5, 8; 1, 2, 3, 6, 7; 1, 2, 4, 5, 7; 1, 3, 4, 5, 6
5	20	1, 2, 3, 5, 9; 1, 2, 3, 6, 8; 1, 2, 4, 5, 8; 1, 2, 4, 6, 7; 1, 3, 4, 5, 7; 2, 3, 4, 5, 6
5	21	1, 2, 3, 6, 9; 1, 2, 3, 7, 8; 1, 2, 4, 5, 9; 1, 2, 4, 6, 8; 1, 2, 5, 6, 7; 1, 3, 4, 5, 8; 1, 3, 4, 6, 7; 2, 3, 4, 5, 7
5	22	1, 2, 3, 7, 9; 1, 2, 4, 6, 9; 1, 2, 4, 7, 8; 1, 2, 5, 6, 8; 1, 3, 4, 5, 9; 1, 3, 4, 6, 8; 1, 3, 5, 6, 7; 2, 3, 4, 5, 8; 2, 3, 4, 6, 7
5	23	1, 2, 3, 8, 9; 1, 2, 4, 7, 9; 1, 2, 5, 6, 9; 1, 2, 5, 7, 8; 1, 3, 4, 6, 9; 1, 3, 4, 7, 8; 1, 3, 5, 6, 8; 1, 4, 5, 6, 7; 2, 3, 4, 5, 9; 2, 3, 4, 6, 8; 2, 3, 5, 6, 7
5	24	1, 2, 4, 8, 9; 1, 2, 5, 7, 9; 1, 2, 6, 7, 8; 1, 3, 4, 7, 9; 1, 3, 5, 6, 9; 1, 3, 5, 7, 8; 1, 4, 5, 6, 8; 2, 3, 4, 6, 9; 2, 3, 4, 7, 8; 2, 3, 5, 6, 8; 2, 4, 5, 6, 7
5	25	1, 2, 5, 8, 9; 1, 2, 6, 7, 9; 1, 3, 4, 8, 9; 1, 3, 5, 7, 9; 1, 3, 6, 7, 8; 1, 4, 5, 6, 9; 1, 4, 5, 7, 8; 2, 3, 4, 7, 9; 2, 3, 5, 6, 9; 2, 3, 5, 7, 8; 2, 4, 5, 6, 8; 3, 4, 5, 6, 7

5	26	1, 2, 6, 8, 9; 1, 3, 5, 8, 9; 1, 3, 6, 7, 9; 1, 4, 5, 7, 9; 1, 4, 6, 7, 8; 2, 3, 4, 8, 9; 2, 3, 5, 7, 9; 2, 3, 6, 7, 8; 2, 4, 5, 6, 9; 2, 4, 5, 7, 8; 3, 4, 5, 6, 8
5	27	1, 2, 7, 8, 9; 1, 3, 6, 8, 9; 1, 4, 5, 8, 9; 1, 4, 6, 7, 9; 1, 5, 6, 7, 8; 2, 3, 5, 8, 9; 2, 3, 6, 7, 9; 2, 4, 5, 7, 9; 2, 4, 6, 7, 8; 3, 4, 5, 6, 9; 3, 4, 5, 7, 8
5	28	1, 3, 7, 8, 9; 1, 4, 6, 8, 9; 1, 5, 6, 7, 9; 2, 3, 6, 8, 9; 2, 4, 5, 8, 9; 2, 4, 6, 7, 9; 2, 5, 6, 7, 8; 3, 4, 5, 7, 9; 3, 4, 6, 7, 8
5	29	1, 4, 7, 8, 9; 1, 5, 6, 8, 9; 2, 3, 7, 8, 9; 2, 4, 6, 8, 9; 2, 5, 6, 7, 9; 3, 4, 5, 8, 9; 3, 4, 6, 7, 9; 3, 5, 6, 7, 8
5	30	1, 5, 7, 8, 9; 2, 4, 7, 8, 9; 2, 5, 6, 8, 9; 3, 4, 6, 8, 9; 3, 5, 6, 7, 9; 4, 5, 6, 7, 8
5	31	1, 6, 7, 8, 9; 2, 5, 7, 8, 9; 3, 4, 7, 8, 9; 3, 5, 6, 8, 9; 4, 5, 6, 7, 9
5	32	2, 6, 7, 8, 9; 3, 5, 7, 8, 9; 4, 5, 6, 8, 9
5	33	3, 6, 7, 8, 9; 4, 5, 7, 8, 9
5	34	4, 6, 7, 8, 9
5	35	5, 6, 7, 8, 9
6	21	1, 2, 3, 4, 5, 6
6	22	1, 2, 3, 4, 5, 7
6	23	1, 2, 3, 4, 5, 8; 1, 2, 3, 4, 6, 7
6	24	1, 2, 3, 4, 5, 9; 1, 2, 3, 4, 6, 8; 1, 2, 3, 5, 6, 7
6	25	1, 2, 3, 4, 6, 9; 1, 2, 3, 4, 7, 8; 1, 2, 3, 5, 6, 8; 1, 2, 4, 5, 6, 7
6	26	1, 2, 3, 4, 7, 9; 1, 2, 3, 5, 6, 9; 1, 2, 3, 5, 7, 8; 1, 2, 4, 5, 6, 8; 1, 3, 4, 5, 6, 7
6	27	1, 2, 3, 4, 8, 9; 1, 2, 3, 5, 7, 9; 1, 2, 3, 6, 7, 8; 1, 2, 4, 5, 6, 9; 1, 2, 4, 5, 7, 8; 1, 3, 4, 5, 6, 8; 2, 3, 4, 5, 6, 7
6	28	1, 2, 3, 5, 8, 9; 1, 2, 3, 6, 7, 9; 1, 2, 4, 5, 7, 9; 1, 2, 4, 6, 7, 8; 1, 3, 4, 5, 6, 9; 1, 3, 4, 5, 7, 8; 2, 3, 4, 5, 6, 8
6	29	1, 2, 3, 6, 8, 9; 1, 2, 4, 5, 8, 9; 1, 2, 4, 6, 7, 9; 1, 2, 5, 6, 7, 8; 1, 3, 4, 5, 7, 9; 1, 3, 4, 6, 7, 8; 2, 3, 4, 5, 6, 9; 2, 3, 4, 5, 7, 8

6	30	1, 2, 3, 7, 8, 9; 1, 2, 4, 6, 8, 9; 1, 2, 5, 6, 7, 9; 1, 3, 4, 5, 8, 9; 1, 3, 4, 6, 7, 9; 1, 3, 5, 6, 7, 8; 2, 3, 4, 5, 7, 9; 2, 3, 4, 6, 7, 8
6	31	1, 2, 4, 7, 8, 9; 1, 2, 5, 6, 8, 9; 1, 3, 4, 6, 8, 9; 1, 3, 5, 6, 7, 9; 1, 4, 5, 6, 7, 8; 2, 3, 4, 5, 8, 9; 2, 3, 4, 6, 7, 9; 2, 3, 5, 6, 7, 8
6	32	1, 2, 5, 7, 8, 9; 1, 3, 4, 7, 8, 9; 1, 3, 5, 6, 8, 9; 1, 4, 5, 6, 7, 9; 2, 3, 4, 6, 8, 9; 2, 3, 5, 6, 7, 9; 2, 4, 5, 6, 7, 8
6	33	1, 2, 6, 7, 8, 9; 1, 3, 5, 7, 8, 9; 1, 4, 5, 6, 8, 9; 2, 3, 4, 7, 8, 9; 2, 3, 5, 6, 8, 9; 2, 4, 5, 6, 7, 9; 3, 4, 5, 6, 7, 8
6	34	1, 3, 6, 7, 8, 9; 1, 4, 5, 7, 8, 9; 2, 3, 5, 7, 8, 9; 2, 4, 5, 6, 8, 9; 3, 4, 5, 6, 7, 9
6	35	1, 4, 6, 7, 8, 9; 2, 3, 6, 7, 8, 9; 2, 4, 5, 7, 8, 9; 3, 4, 5, 6, 8, 9
6	36	1, 5, 6, 7, 8, 9; 2, 4, 6, 7, 8, 9; 3, 4, 5, 7, 8, 9
6	37	2, 5, 6, 7, 8, 9; 3, 4, 6, 7, 8, 9
6	38	3, 5, 6, 7, 8, 9
6	39	4, 5, 6, 7, 8, 9
7	28	1, 2, 3, 4, 5, 6, 7
7	29	1, 2, 3, 4, 5, 6, 8
7	30	1, 2, 3, 4, 5, 6, 9; 1, 2, 3, 4, 5, 7, 8
7	31	1, 2, 3, 4, 5, 7, 9; 1, 2, 3, 4, 6, 7, 8
7	32	1, 2, 3, 4, 5, 8, 9; 1, 2, 3, 4, 6, 7, 9; 1, 2, 3, 5, 6, 7, 8
7	33	1, 2, 3, 4, 6, 8, 9; 1, 2, 3, 5, 6, 7, 9; 1, 2, 4, 5, 6, 7, 8
7	34	1, 2, 3, 4, 7, 8, 9; 1, 2, 3, 5, 6, 8, 9; 1, 2, 4, 5, 6, 7, 9; 1, 3, 4, 5, 6, 7, 8
7	35	1, 2, 3, 5, 7, 8, 9; 1, 2, 4, 5, 6, 8, 9; 1, 3, 4, 5, 6, 7, 9; 2, 3, 4, 5, 6, 7, 8
7	36	1, 2, 3, 6, 7, 8, 9; 1, 2, 4, 5, 7, 8, 9; 1, 3, 4, 5, 6, 8, 9; 2, 3, 4, 5, 6, 7, 9
7	37	1, 2, 4, 6, 7, 8, 9; 1, 3, 4, 5, 7, 8, 9; 2, 3, 4, 5, 6, 8, 9

7	38	1, 2, 5, 6, 7, 8, 9; 1, 3, 4, 6, 7, 8, 9; 2, 3, 4, 5, 7, 8, 9
7	39	1, 3, 5, 6, 7, 8, 9; 2, 3, 4, 6, 7, 8, 9
7	40	1, 4, 5, 6, 7, 8, 9; 2, 3, 5, 6, 7, 8, 9
7	41	2, 4, 5, 6, 7, 8, 9
7	42	3, 4, 5, 6, 7, 8, 9
8	36	1, 2, 3, 4, 5, 6, 7, 8
8	37	1, 2, 3, 4, 5, 6, 7, 9
8	38	1, 2, 3, 4, 5, 6, 8, 9
8	39	1, 2, 3, 4, 5, 7, 8, 9
8	40	1, 2, 3, 4, 6, 7, 8, 9
8	41	1, 2, 3, 5, 6, 7, 8, 9
8	42	1, 2, 4, 5, 6, 7, 8, 9
8	43	1, 3, 4, 5, 6, 7, 8, 9
8	44	2, 3, 4, 5, 6, 7, 8, 9
9	45	1, 2, 3, 4, 5, 6, 7, 8, 9

Printed in the United States
by Baker & Taylor Publisher Services